PARA MI PEQUEÑO NOAH, TE QUIERO GORDITO

SPANISH MADE SIMPLE

OMAR ALLIBHOY

SPANISH MADE SIMPLE

FOOLPROOF SPANISH RECIPES FOR EVERY DAY

OMAR ALLIBHOY

PHOTOGRAPHY BY MARTIN POOLE

Hardie Grant

QUADRILLE

TABLA DE CONTENIDOS
CONTENTS

INTRODUCTION

In this book I want to introduce you to the home-cooked meals that are widely enjoyed in my country, Spain, the food I grew up eating and that I cook every day at home, the dinners that made our gastronomy so famous. My philosophy in the kitchen has always been the same: cook without fuss and eat like a king – quite simply. Eating great food is a luxury we all have the right to, so make the most of it.

I have a passion for Spanish food and tapas which I love to share – so much so that it has become my mission in life. I have felt this way ever since I left my beloved Madrid over a decade ago and I was exposed to other cuisines.

As a chef I had the pleasure and honour in my early years of training with and learning from some of the most talented chefs such as Ferran Adrià and Gordon Ramsay... As a diner I have travelled and eaten across dozens of countries, visited their restaurants, learned how they cook – but more importantly experienced how locals eat daily in their own homes with their loved ones.

It was on these travels that I began to realize how incredible, generous and tasty the food I grew up with was compared to the food I was discovering all over the world. Don't get me wrong: I love all food, but the dishes one grows up with leave an indelible mark on your heart, from the flavours, aromas and memories around them, to – in my case – the quick and easy dinners my mum used to rustle up in minutes, and the bigger family feasts where great conversation and laughter were vital ingredients around the table. Invariably, the most vivid memories of my life have centred around food with my family and friends.

Spain has a huge influx of tourists. I know I am a bit biased, but its popularity isn't surprising to me, as it's a sunny country blessed with beautiful and varied geography and landscapes, historically fascinating cities, stunning gastronomy and generally very funny and outgoing people with the greatest lifestyles. However, essentially what makes us all happy is not a location, the way the streets look or the weather, but actually the culture and lifestyle that we live and enjoy.

Working abroad for so long and running my own Spanish restaurants have given me the opportunity to appreciate the kinship so many people feel for my country when they first visit, which then turns into love when they come for the second time. This is the type of response that makes me very proud of my people and feel lucky about where I grew up.

I have experienced first-hand how much everyone loves our food and tapas, no matter where they themselves come from; it's the first thing they talk about when you ask them about Spain. I have concluded that food is one of the most important things in making a culture what it is because of how much pleasure we get from it and what it means to all of us.

I hope all this articulates why I am so passionate about Spanish food and why I have the urge to share it with you. My aim is to convince you to add some of my favourite dishes to your weekly repertoire.

Inside these pages you will find the best recipes I have to offer, for all sorts of occasions including quick midweek suppers, weekend lunches, full-on evening gatherings and of course some tapas. They have all been translated from my Spanish kitchen where most of the recipes are unwritten; they are just passed on verbally from generation to generation. They are authentic and simple – but some have necessitated a few phone calls to my mum and aunty, I must confess!

Food changes a lot through every season and every province across Spain to suit both the local climate and produce. This is part of the beauty of the country – with such a wealth of variety, it feels like our gastronomy has infinite potential. The following recipes hail from every corner, from the hot Andalucía to the cooler Galicia, passing through historic Castilla and all the Mediterranean coast. I hope you'll find it a journey of discovery through the best-tasting and most authentic dishes.

I have tried to describe the recipes vividly and portray them as simply as I could so that no method, technique or ingredient sounds alien to anyone. You will find some shortcuts of the kind that I often employ at home, because unfortunately time is of the essence at Casa Allibhoy, too!

Buen provecho.
Omar

DE APERITIVO

{ NIBBLES }

⋆ SANGRIA DE CAVA ⋆

SANGRIA MADE WITH SPANISH SPARKLING WINE

MAKES 2 LITRES (2 QUARTS)

1 ORANGE

200G (1 CUP) SOFT BROWN SUGAR

1 CINNAMON STICK

10 STRAWBERRIES, QUARTERED

1 PEAR, CORED AND ROUGHLY CHOPPED

1 PEACH, ROUGHLY CHOPPED

200ML (¾ CUP) BRANDY

200ML (¾ CUP) COINTREAU

1 X 75CL BOTTLE SPANISH CAVA BRUT

FRESH MINT LEAVES

Cava is made in the same way as champagne. Not many sparkling wines use the same method and, to me, champagne and cava definitely have the edge over prosecco or other sparkling wines. Cava has always been a celebration drink in Spain, but with prices being so affordable these days I thought I could make a sangria with it. The result is so refreshing, fruity and sharp.

Refrigerate your glasses so that you can enjoy your drink as cold as possible.

Remove the zest of the orange in long strips. Squeeze the juice into a saucepan with the strips of zest, the sugar, cinnamon stick, the strawberries and the chopped pear and peach. Bring to the boil and cook for 1 minute. Pour into a 2-litre jug (2-quart pitcher) with the brandy and Cointreau, stir with a wooden spoon and put in the fridge to chill until completely cold.

Stir the chilled mixture again and then pour 3 Tbsp into each glass. Top up with the fizzy cava, serve with a mint leaf and enjoy it while it lasts.

★ BUÑUELOS DE BACALAO ★

SALT COD FRITTERS

SERVES 8

125G (4½OZ) BONELESS AND SKINLESS DRIED SALT COD (BACALAO) (YOU CAN USE JUST FRESH COD IF YOU PREFER, BUT YOU WILL LOSE A LOT OF THE INTENSITY OF FLAVOUR)

2 POTATOES (ABOUT 650G [1½LB])

200G (7OZ) FRESH COD

2 TBSP FINELY CHOPPED CHIVES

1 GARLIC CLOVE, CRUSHED

1 WHOLE EGG + 1 EGG YOLK

SUNFLOWER OIL, FOR DEEP-FRYING

ALIOLI (SEE PAGE 27) OR ROMESCO SAUCE (SEE PAGE 100), TO SERVE

Traditional *buñuelos* used to be sweet and were commonly sold in bakeries at Easter time. With time, more developed recipes have arisen to bring us *buñuelos* made with savoury ingredients, such as cod (*bacalao*), cheese or even chard. These salt cod and cheese (see recipe on page 14) versions – both pictured here – are totally different; I urge you to try them both as they are seriously good.

First, to rehydrate the salt cod, put it in a container and pour in enough cold water to cover. Leave overnight and change the water at least twice to extract as much salt as possible from the cod.

When you are ready to start cooking, peel and cut the potatoes into 1-cm (⅜-in) thick slices. Boil in unsalted water over a medium heat for about 15 minutes, or until cooked through. Drain and allow to dry.

Finely chop both the rehydrated salt cod and the fresh cod, removing any bones you find. Mix with the chives and garlic by hand or using a blender or food processor. Add the egg, egg yolk and boiled potatoes and mash together. Set aside for at least 10 minutes while you heat the oil. Depending on the potato and the size of your eggs, the mixture could be a bit loose. If so, add 1 Tbsp plain (all-purpose) flour and it should be better.

Pour enough oil into a deep pan to cover the base by about 3cm (1¼in). Heat until a cube of day-old bread dropped into the oil turns golden in about 30 seconds. Alternatively, heat a deep fryer to 180°C (360°F).

Pour tablespoonfuls of the mixture into the hot oil and fry until they float and turn light golden, up to 2 minutes. Remove from the oil with a slotted spoon and drain on kitchen paper while you finish the fritters. Serve with Alioli or Romesco Sauce.

★ BUÑUELOS DE QUESO ★

CHEESE FRITTERS

SERVES 8

45G (3½ TBSP) BUTTER

2G (½ TSP) TABLE SALT

75G (9 TBSP) PLAIN
(ALL-PURPOSE) FLOUR

3 EGGS

50G (½ CUP) GRATED MANCHEGO
OR CHEDDAR CHEESE

1 GARLIC CLOVE, FINELY CHOPPED

1 SPRING ONION (SCALLION),
THINLY SLICED

VEGETABLE OIL, FOR DEEP-FRYING

ALIOLI (SEE PAGE 27) OR ROMESCO
SAUCE (SEE PAGE 100), TO SERVE

Place 100ml (⅓ cup + 1 Tbsp) water, the butter and salt in a pan and bring to the boil. Add the flour, remove from the heat and mix with a wooden spoon for about 30 seconds until it is well combined and the mixture has become a ball that pulls away from the sides of the pan. Take off the heat.

Add the eggs, one at a time, stirring each one into the dough completely before adding the next one. The mixture should have the consistency of thick yogurt at this point. Add the grated cheese, garlic and spring onion and mix until well combined.

Pour enough oil into a deep pan to cover the base by about 3cm (1¼in). Heat until a cube of day-old bread dropped into the oil turns golden in about 30 seconds. Alternatively, heat a deep fryer to 180°C (360°F).

Use a couple of spoons to start dropping in knobs of dough about the size of a walnut. The dough should start frying and puff up immediately and after a few seconds they will turn over by themselves. Leave them in the oil until they turn golden brown, about 2 minutes, then scoop out with a slotted spoon and drain on kitchen paper. Cook in batches so that the oil doesn't cool down too much. Your *buñuelos* should have a delicate crispness on the outside and be pretty much all air on the inside. Serve with Alioli or Romesco Sauce.

★ PATATAS BRAVAS ★

FRIED POTATOES WITH SPICY TOMATO SAUCE

SERVES 4 AS A TAPA

2–3 LARGE MARIS PIPER OR OTHER
FLOURY POTATOES, PEELED

MILD OLIVE OR SUNFLOWER OIL,
FOR DEEP-FRYING

OR

OLIVE OIL, A FEW ROSEMARY SPRIGS,
A FEW CRUSHED GARLIC CLOVES,
SALT AND FRESHLY GROUND BLACK
PEPPER, FOR ROASTING

ALIOLI, TO SERVE (SEE PAGE 27)

FOR THE SAUCE

1 GARLIC CLOVE, THINLY SLICED

½ ONION, THINLY SLICED

2 DRIED CAYENNE CHILLI PEPPERS
(THIS IS ENOUGH, I SWEAR)

½ BAY LEAF

1 TBSP WHITE VINEGAR

A PINCH OF DRIED OREGANO

A PINCH OF GROUND CUMIN

250ML (1 CUP) TOMATO PASSATA
(OR STRAINED OR MILLED
CANNED TOMATOES)

I was born in Madrid, hence I love my *patatas bravas*, a real staple tapa where I come from. You will find endless recipes and styles for the same dish; in some places they are served with alioli mixed with the spicy sauce. It is definitely one of the more simple and typical tapa of our gastronomy, and the most popular in all my tapas bars.

Sauté the garlic and onion for the sauce in a pan over a medium heat with the cayenne peppers and bay leaf until the onion is soft (about 20 minutes). Add the vinegar, oregano and cumin, let the mixture boil for 30 seconds and then add the passata. Cook for a further 15 minutes. Set aside to cool a little, then blend until silky-smooth.

For the potatoes, it could be as simple as cutting them into wedges. Now, I like my *bravas* cut in irregular wedges, let's say about 2.5cm (1in) big. However you choose to cut them, put them into a pan of cold water, bring them to the boil and then cook for about 15 minutes, until soft. Drain and leave to dry completely.

Pour enough oil into a deep pan to fill it to about a third full. Heat until a cube of day-old bread dropped into the oil turns golden in about 30 seconds. Alternatively, heat a deep fryer to 180°C (360°F). Cook half the potatoes for about 5 minutes to create the crunchy outer crust. Repeat with the rest of the potatoes. Alternatively, roast the potatoes for 20 minutes at 200°C/400°F/gas mark 6, with a bit of olive oil, a few rosemary sprigs, a few crushed garlic cloves, salt and pepper. The result is also very good.

Serve the cooked potatoes with the warm sauce poured over the top. You could also add a spoonful of Alioli. A refreshing cold beer is my suggestion to match this tapa and to cope with the hot sauce!

EMPANADILLAS
★ DE QUESO Y ESPINACA ★

PASTRY PARCELS FILLED WITH SPINACH, RAISINS AND GOAT CHEESE

SERVES 8 AS A TAPA

FOR THE DOUGH

75ML (⅓ CUP) OLIVE OIL

175G (1⅓ CUPS) PLAIN
(ALL-PURPOSE) FLOUR

A PINCH OF SALT

1 EGG, BEATEN

FOR THE FILLING

5 TBSP OLIVE OIL

1 ONION, THINLY SLICED

2 GARLIC CLOVES, FINELY CHOPPED

3 TBSP RAISINS

200G (SCANT 4 CUPS) BABY
SPINACH (OR USE FROZEN)

50G (2OZ) GOAT CHEESE

A PINCH OF SALT

A PINCH OF WHITE PEPPER

2 TBSP DOUBLE (HEAVY) CREAM

NOTE
These can also be
shallow-fried in oil
over a medium heat for
2 minutes on each side.

I grew up eating these (like every Spanish kid really) but traditionally they tend to be filled with tuna, red (bell) peppers and tomato. This vegetarian version is so tasty and so popular in my restaurants.

To make the dough, pour the oil and 75ml (⅓ cup water) into a saucepan over a high heat and bring to the boil. Take off the heat and add the flour and salt, stirring vigorously for about 1 minute, until fully mixed. Allow to cool a little, then knead for 1 minute. Wrap in plastic wrap and refrigerate for 30 minutes.

Roll out the chilled pastry on a lightly floured surface to about 3mm (⅛in) thick and cut out as many circles as you can using a saucer as a template. Re-roll the scraps to make more circles. Set aside.

Pour the olive oil for the filling into a large frying pan and gently fry the onion over a medium heat for a good 20 minutes until golden. Add the garlic and raisins and fry with the onion for a further 5 minutes. Add the spinach, crumble in the goat cheese and season with the salt and pepper. Let it all wilt and melt for a couple of minutes and then add the cream. Don't leave it over the heat for longer than 2 minutes. Refrigerate for at least 30 minutes so that it becomes easier to handle.

Preheat the oven to 200°C/400°F/gas mark 6.

Spread the pastry discs over the worktop and add a tablespoon of the filling to each one. Brush all around the edges with the beaten egg, then fold each one over to make semi-circles. Use a fork to press the edges together to seal. Brush each *empanadilla* with more egg and bake for 10 minutes, or until golden and crispy.

See photograph on page 8.

★ CHAMPIÑONES GRATINADOS ★

MUSHROOM GRATIN WITH HAM MAYONNAISE

SERVES 4 AS A TAPA

4 PORTOBELLO MUSHROOMS, STALKS TRIMMED

2 SPRIGS FRESH THYME, LEAVES SEPARATED

OLIVE OIL

THE GREEN PART OF 1 SPRING ONION (SCALLION), FINELY CHOPPED

SEA SALT AND FRESHLY GROUND BLACK PEPPER

FOR THE HAM MAYONNAISE

1 EGG YOLK

1 GARLIC CLOVE

A PINCH OF SALT

1 TBSP LEMON JUICE OR VINEGAR

3 SLICES SERRANO HAM, ROUGHLY CHOPPED

150ML (⅔ CUP) MILD OLIVE OIL

This simple recipe carries an explosion of flavour. It makes a great starter (appetizer) when you are entertaining friends or family, as you can leave it hot in the oven until you need it. I use portobello mushrooms but you can use any flat mushroom, or even large oyster types.

Place the mushrooms on a roasting tray and sprinkle with sea salt, a bit of black pepper, the fresh thyme leaves and a drizzle of olive oil. Place in a cold oven and set the temperature to 180°C/350°F/gas mark 4. Bake for 15 minutes.

Meanwhile, for the ham mayonnaise, blend the egg yolk, garlic clove, salt, lemon juice and ham in a food processor and then start to add the oil in a steady stream until you have a mayonnaise.

Remove the tray from the oven and sprinkle the mushrooms with the chopped spring onion. Top with a dollop of the ham mayonnaise and return to the oven for a good 5 minutes, or until the top has nicely browned.

See photographs on following pages.

★ TOSTA DE HIGOS CON JAMON ★

PAN-FRIED FIGS, SERRANO HAM, CREAM CHEESE
AND WALNUTS ON TOAST

SERVES 4 AS A TAPA

100G (½ CUP) CREAM CHEESE

50G (½ CUP) WALNUT HALVES

4 SLICES RUSTIC BREAD, TOASTED

8 FIGS

EXTRA VIRGIN OLIVE OIL

1 TBSP BROWN SUGAR

A SPLASH OF SHERRY VINEGAR

A PINCH OF ROCK OR SEA SALT

8 THIN SLICES SERRANO HAM

NOTE
Try this recipe with
melon instead of figs –
it will be equally great.

Tapas are much easier to make at home than people think, and these days you can find most Spanish ingredients in your local supermarket so there is no excuse. Figs are at their peak in early autumn; make sure you buy soft and sweet ones.

Mix the cream cheese with three-quarters of the walnuts, crumbling them between your hands and beating them into the cheese with a fork. Spread generously over the bread.

Open your figs by cutting a cross at the pointed end and opening them out like a flower with your fingers.

Drizzle some olive oil into a pan over a medium heat and add the brown sugar. Add the figs and fry the bases only, without turning them; we only want to cook the bottoms of the figs. Watch that the caramel that forms in the pan doesn't burn. Add the sherry vinegar and turn off the heat.

Place your hot figs over the toasts and drizzle with the hot vinaigrette from the pan. Top with a good drizzle of extra virgin olive oil, a pinch of salt and the slices of Serrano ham. Sprinkle with the remaining walnuts.

ANCHOAS SALADAS
★ CON VINAGRE Y PIMENTON ★

SALTED ANCHOVIES WITH PAPRIKA AND VINEGAR

SERVES 3 AS AN APERITIVO

1 X 50-G TIN (2-OZ CAN) SALTED ANCHOVIES (OR SARDINES) IN OIL

3 TBSP EXTRA VIRGIN OLIVE OIL

A PINCH OF SWEET PIMENTÓN (SWEET SMOKED PAPRIKA)

1 TBSP SHERRY VINEGAR

1 BAG OF PLAIN CRISPS (POTATO CHIPS), TO SERVE

You probably wouldn't imagine that a salted anchovy could actually be marinated. You will be very surprised by how much it can change with just this small touch, and for the better!

Drain the oil from the anchovies.

Mix together the extra virgin olive oil with the pimentón and vinegar and pour over the anchovies. Let them marinate for 5 minutes and enjoy each anchovy on top of a crisp, as it is a tradition in tapas bars across Spain.

★ BANDERILLAS ★

SKEWERED PICKLES

MAKES AS MANY AS YOU LIKE!

WHITE OR SALTED ANCHOVIES

GREEN SPANISH QUEEN OLIVES

GREEN CHILLI PEPPERS IN BRINE
(PREFERABLY HOT SPANISH GREEN)

PICKLED SILVER (PEARL OR BABY)
ONIONS

GHERKINS

EXTRA VIRGIN OLIVE OIL

18-CM (7-IN) WOODEN SKEWERS
OR STRONG COCKTAIL STICKS
(TOOTHPICKS)

Pickled *banderillas* – customized skewers with your favourite pickles – are another ubiquitous tapa in bars around Spain. We love all pickles; in our supermarkets you will find a wide range of brined vegetables from garlic to artichokes, and fish, from mussels to anchovies. The vinegar flavour tastes exciting in your mouth and it is the perfect match for a beer or two, as an *aperitivo*. In Spain you can find *banderillas* ready made, but we prefer to make them ourselves and choose the ingredients we fancy.

Roll an anchovy around an olive and poke a skewer through the middle, getting both sides of the fish and making sure they are well stacked. Next, introduce a chilli pepper. Because they are normally quite long, I recommend you cut it in half or fold it over. Follow this with a baby onion and lastly, introduce the gherkin. This ingredient should not be missing in any combination; it is the main pickle of the *banderilla*. Prick the gherkin horizontally. Of course, you can change the order of the ingredients, as you like.

Repeat to make all the skewers you require. Pour over a drizzle of extra virgin olive oil and serve.

★ HUEVOS RELLENOS DE ATUN ★

TUNA-STUFFED EGGS

SERVES 4 AS A TAPA

4 EGGS

2 TSP TOMATO KETCHUP

1 DROP TABASCO SAUCE

2 DROPS WORCESTERSHIRE SAUCE

A PINCH OF SALT

1 X 160-G TIN (6-OZ CAN) TUNA
IN BRINE OR OIL, DRAINED
AND SHREDDED

**FOR THE MAYONNAISE
(MAKES ABOUT 250G [1 CUP]),
OR SERVES 8**

1 EGG

JUICE OF ½ LEMON

1 TSP SALT

200ML (¾ CUP) MILD OLIVE OIL

Back in my country, we love to have our birthday parties at home and you will find these finger foods at all these family celebrations.

Place the eggs in boiling water and cook for exactly 6 minutes, then run under cold water. Peel the eggs and halve them. Remove the yolks, mush them with a fork and set aside both parts of the eggs.

For the mayonnaise, take a glass jar wide enough to fit a hand blender and pour all the ingredients into it. Let them sit for 1 minute. Now put the hand blender in the bottom of the jar and blend – the egg and lemon juice will emulsify first. Slowly lift the hand blender up through the ingredients for about 30 seconds – the oil will emulsify at this stage and your mayonnaise will not split. This is exactly how mayonnaise is made in Spain!

Mix together 2 tablespoons of the mayonnaise, the ketchup, Tabasco, Worcestershire sauce and salt. Add the shredded tuna, give it a good stir and then add the yolks and mix again.

Use a teaspoon to fill the empty boiled egg white halves with the tuna mixture and serve.

GARLIC MAYONNAISE

**MAKES ABOUT 250G (1 CUP),
OR SERVES 8**

1 EGG

2 GARLIC CLOVES

1 TBSP LEMON JUICE

½ TSP SALT

100ML (⅓ CUP + 1 TBSP)
VEGETABLE OIL

100ML (⅓ CUP + 1 TBSP)
EXTRA VIRGIN OLIVE OIL

Alioli is such a versatile sauce that combines well with so many dishes. It can be fine-tuned to incorporate a distinctive flavour and accompany specific types of food, for example saffron, lime, pimentón – you name it.

Put the egg, garlic, lemon juice, salt and a drizzle of either oil in a small jug. Using a stick blender, blitz all the ingredients together. With the blender still going, very slowly trickle in the remaining oils until they have all been added and the alioli has completely emulsified.

If you are unlucky enough that your alioli splits, just start again with a bit of water in the jug before pouring the split mixture into it and blitzing it again.

VARIATIONS

Alioli can be turned into something completely different and become a key ingredient in its own right if blended with some more substantial extras. This is a popular technique in Spain when making canapés at home, or at least in my family, where we add grated Manchego cheese in generous amounts and spread it on toast. Another good variation is to add some finely chopped mussels preserved in escabeche or cockles in brine, then fill vols au vent or tartlets with the alioli and sprinkle some snipped chives on top.

★ BOCADILLOS VARIADOS ★

ASSORTED SANDWICHES

These are Spanish takes on regular sandwiches, perfect for any occasion:
a picnic, to bring to work, to a football match, for school... Actually, when
I was a kid we had a healthy competition at school to see who brought in
the best *bocadillo* every day for the break.

MAKES 1

A DRIZZLE OF OLIVE OIL

A SMALL KNOB OF BUTTER

½ SMALL ONION, FINELY CHOPPED

1 SMALL RUSTIC CIABATTA BREAD,
SLICED IN HALF

SOBRASADA DE MALLORCA
(SEE PAGE 84) OR 5 CHORIZO SLICES

1 TSP HONEY

30G (1OZ) CHEDDAR, THINLY SLICED

ALMUSSAFES

CHORIZO PATE AND CHEESE SANDWICH

Heat the oil and butter in a pan over a medium heat
and add the onion. Cook for about 10 minutes until
soft and golden. Set aside. Toast the bread halves in the
same pan. Spread one of the halves with the sobrasada,
or lay the chorizo slices over the top, and drizzle with
the honey. Top with the caramelized onion and cheese.
Close the sandwich and be happy.

MAKES 1

A SMALL KNOB OF BUTTER

1 SMALL RUSTIC CIABATTA BREAD,
SLICED IN HALF

2 THIN BEEF STEAKS, PREFERABLY
SIRLOIN (STRIP STEAK) OR
BAVETTE (FLAP MEAT)

SALT AND FRESHLY GROUND
BLACK PEPPER

CHIPS (FRIES) TO SERVE, OPTIONAL

PEPITO DE TERNERA

BEEF SANDWICH

Melt the butter in a pan over a medium heat and fry
the bread. Set aside. Put the steak in the same pan over
a high heat, season with salt and pepper and cook to
your liking. Assemble the sandwich and enjoy freshly
made with some chips on the side, if you like.

See photographs on pages 30 and 31.

> **NOTE**
> This sandwich
> doesn't travel well!

MEDIA LUNA DE ATUN Y ALIOLI

**TUNA AND ALIOLI SANDWICH
WITH PIQUILLO PEPPERS**

MAKES 1

1 BRIOCHE ROLL OR 'PAIN AU LAIT',
SLICED IN HALF

1 TBSP TINNED TUNA IN OIL, DRAINED

2 TBSP ALIOLI (SEE PAGE 27)
OR MAYONNAISE (SEE PAGE 26)

2 COOKED WHITE ASPARAGUS
FROM A TIN/JAR, HALVED

1 PIQUILLO PEPPER, SLICED
IN HALF LENGTHWAYS

A SPRINKLING OF SHREDDED LETTUCE

Toast the roll halves over a hot pan or under a grill (broiler). Mix the tuna with the Alioli or Mayonnaise and spread it over one half of the brioche. Top with the asparagus, piquillo pepper and lettuce. Close the roll and serve.

BOCADILLO DE CALAMARES

DEEP-FRIED SQUID SANDWICH

MAKES 1

VEGETABLE OIL, FOR DEEP-FRYING

100G (3½OZ) FROZEN SQUID TUBE,
THINLY SLICED INTO RINGS OR STRIPS

2 TBSP PLAIN (ALL-PURPOSE) FLOUR

1 MINI BAGUETTE, SLICED IN HALF

2 TBSP MAYONNAISE (SEE PAGE 26)

SALT

This is a truly Madrileño speciality. It sounds crazy but when I go to Madrid to visit the family, I can't leave without having one of these.

Pour enough oil into a deep pan to cover the base by about 3cm (1¼in). Heat until a cube of day-old bread dropped into the oil turns golden in about 30 seconds. Alternatively, heat a deep fryer to 180°C (360°F).

Lightly coat the squid in the flour and drop loosely into the hot oil. Fry for about 90 seconds or until crispy. Drain and season with salt. Spread one half of the baguette with a bit of Mayonnaise before stuffing the squid into it. Enjoy hot.

BOCADILLO DE JAMON IBERICO

ACORN-FED-HAM SANDWICH

MAKES 1

2 CHERRY TOMATOES, HALVED

1 MINI BAGUETTE, SLICED IN HALF

A DRIZZLE OF EXTRA VIRGIN OLIVE OIL

A PINCH OF SEA SALT

40G (1½OZ) THINLY SLICED JAMÓN
IBÉRICO (PREFERABLY ACORN-FED)

Squeeze the cherry tomatoes and rub them over the inside of the bread. Drizzle generously with the olive oil, sprinkle with a touch of the sea salt and lay the ham on the bread. This particular sandwich should have a space in heaven.

See photographs on following pages.

★ COCA DE REQUENA ★

MEAT FOCACCIA

SERVES 6

FOR THE DOUGH

7G (SCANT 1 TSP) DRIED YEAST

230ML (1 CUP) WARM WATER

300G (2 CUPS + 2 TBSP) STRONG
WHITE BREAD FLOUR

110ML (½ CUP + 2½ TBSP) OLIVE OIL

3G (HEAPED ½ TSP) SALT

FOR THE TOPPINGS

1 CHORIZO COOKING
SAUSAGE, CHOPPED

2 PORK SAUSAGES, CHOPPED

3 SLICES STREAKY BACON
OR PANCETTA, CUT IN HALF

2 SLICES BLACK PUDDING (BLOOD
SAUSAGE), CHOPPED, OPTIONAL

Across Spain we combine a variety of leavened breads, rolls and flatbreads with other ingredients. This version reminds me of a British 'toad in the hole', but made with a focaccia-like bread instead of batter. All the rendered fats from the meats are absorbed into the bread, resulting in a very indulgent experience.

First make the dough. In a large bowl, mix together the yeast and warm water and stir until dissolved. Mix the flour with the oil and salt and tip this into the bowl. Knead for at least 6–8 minutes, until you can bring the dough together with your hands. Cover with a cloth and allow to rest at room temperature for 1 hour.

Preheat the oven to 200°C/400°F/gas mark 6.

Dust a work surface with flour and roll out the dough to a square about 2cm (¾in) thick and place it on a baking sheet. Top with the chorizo, sausages, bacon and black pudding, if using, and press them gently into the dough.

Bake for about 16 minutes, until the bread has risen and looks crisp and golden and the toppings have released their fats. Tear into pieces at the table.

CARNES Y CAZA

{ MEAT & GAME }

★ CORDERO AL CHILINDRON ★

SLOW-COOKED LAMB AND PEPPER STEW

SERVES 4

1KG (2LB 3OZ) DICED LAMB

A PINCH OF GROUND CUMIN

100G (¾ CUP) PLAIN
(ALL-PURPOSE) FLOUR

175ML (¾ CUP) OLIVE OIL

2 LARGE CARROTS,
CUT INTO THIN STRIPS

1 LARGE ONION, CUT INTO THIN STRIPS

3 GARLIC CLOVES, THINLY SLICED

1 RED (BELL) PEPPER, CUT INTO
THIN STRIPS

½ GREEN (BELL) PEPPER,
CUT INTO THIN STRIPS

A FEW BAY LEAVES

1 SPRIG FRESH THYME,
PLUS EXTRA TO GARNISH

4 TOMATOES, PEELED AND CHOPPED

A PINCH OF SUGAR

1 TSP SWEET PIMENTÓN
(SWEET SMOKED PAPRIKA)

200ML (¾ CUP) WHITE WINE

SALT AND FRESHLY GROUND
BLACK PEPPER

FRIED DICED POTATOES, TO SERVE

This dish is commonly found in northern Spain and was always cooked in the spring with the new lamb season. It's one of those ugly brown but very tasty slow-cooked stews Spain is famous for. We also use other meats for this dish, such as goat or chicken.

Season the lamb with the salt, pepper and just a little pinch of ground cumin, then coat with the flour. Heat the olive oil in a shallow frying pan and toss the coated lamb in the pan for about 5 minutes to seal the edges. Remove the lamb, leaving the oil in the pan, and set it aside to rest.

Add the carrots, onion, garlic and peppers to the cooking oil along with the bay leaves and thyme and reduce the heat to medium. Cook for 10 minutes and then add the chopped tomatoes with the sugar and cook for a further 5 minutes, until the ingredients are combined to make a tomato paste, or *sofrito*.

Add the lamb back to the pan with the sweet pimentón, white wine and 1 litre (4 cups) water and cook over a low heat for a couple of hours, or until the meat is tender, adding more water if necessary. The result should be a rich, dense and silky sauce. Garnish with fresh thyme and serve with fried diced potatoes.

CHULETITAS DE
★ CORDERO MARINADAS ★
MOORISH MARINATED LAMB CUTLETS

SERVES 4 AS A MAIN OR 8 AS A TAPA

12 LAMB CUTLETS
(FRENCH RIBBED CHOPS)

2 GARLIC CLOVES, FINELY CHOPPED

10 SPRIGS FRESH THYME,
LEAVES REMOVED

200ML (1⅓ CUPS) OLIVE OIL

1 TBSP HONEY

2 TSP GROUND CUMIN

2 TSP DRIED OREGANO

1 TSP SWEET OR HOT PIMENTÓN
(SWEET OR HOT SMOKED PAPRIKA)

A PINCH OF SALT

FRESHLY GROUND BLACK PEPPER

FRISÉE LETTUCE, POMEGRANATE
AND OLIVE SALAD (SEE PAGE 140),
TO SERVE, OPTIONAL

These Moorish spiced lamb cutlets are to die for. You can actually use any meat to prepare this dish, such as pork chops or chicken drumsticks. The key is in the marinade. If you are planning a barbecue, don't overlook this recipe.

Place all the ingredients except the meat in a large mixing bowl. Whisk until well combined, then pour the marinade over the lamb cutlets, making sure they are well coated. Marinate for at least 1 hour or up to 2 days in the fridge.

Remove any excess oil from the meat and cook on a very hot dry griddle or frying pan for 2 minutes on each side if you like your meat pink, or 4 minutes if you like it well done. Take care not to burn the outsides. You could also cook them over charcoal or under the grill (broiler) for 10 minutes.

If you're serving as a main meal this works really well alongside the Frisée Lettuce, Pomegranate and Olive Salad.

MACARRONES
★ CON TOMATE Y CHORIZO ★
PENNE PASTA WITH CHORIZO AND TOMATO SAUCE

SERVES 4

1 SMALL ONION, CHOPPED

2 GARLIC CLOVES, SLICED

1 CHORIZO SAUSAGE, DICED

50ML (3⅓ CUP) OLIVE OIL

2 X 400-G TINS (3¼ CUPS)
CHOPPED TOMATOES

1 TSP DRIED OREGANO

1 TBSP SUGAR

350G (12OZ) PENNE PASTA

SALT, OPTIONAL

A SPRINKLING OF GRATED
PARMESAN, TO SERVE

This dish is so popular back home, to the extent that it was a school meal when I was a kid. The chorizo sausage makes a wonderful and rich tomato sauce that, combined with the penne pasta and cheese, turns this into a great lunch or dinner.

Place the onion, garlic, chorizo and olive oil in a large pan over a medium heat. Cook for about 5 minutes, until the onion is soft and the chorizo has released its juices. Add the chopped tomatoes, oregano and sugar and cook until the sauce is rich and has reduced by at least two-thirds. Taste and add salt if needed.

Bring 2 litres (2 quarts) water to the boil, then add the pasta. Cook following the manufacturer's instructions, but drain 2 minutes before the time is over, then add the pasta to the tomato sauce with 100ml (⅓ cup) of the cooking water. Give it a good stir over a high heat to mix all the ingredients thoroughly. Serve with a sprinkling of grated Parmesan cheese.

TORREZNOS
★ CON MOJO DULCE ★

SLOW-COOKED PORK BELLY WITH A SWEET, SPICY AND SOUR SAUCE

SERVES 4

1KG (2LB 3OZ) PORK BELLY

1 TBSP ROCK SALT

250ML (1 CUP) WHITE WINE OR BEER

600G (1LB 5OZ) NEW POTATOES

FOR THE MOJO DULCE SAUCE

6 DRIED CAYENNE OR BIRD'S EYE CHILLI PEPPERS, FINELY CHOPPED

10G (1 TBSP + 2 TSP) GROUND CUMIN

10G (1 TBSP + 2 TSP) SWEET PIMENTÓN (SWEET SMOKED PAPRIKA)

10G (1 TBSP + 2 TSP) BLACK PEPPER POWDER

5G (1 TBSP + 2 TSP) GROUND CINNAMON

10G (¼ CUP + 2 TBSP) DRIED OREGANO

5G (1 TSP) SALT

75ML (⅓ CUP) SHERRY VINEGAR

50ML (3½ TBSP) EXTRA VIRGIN OLIVE OIL

150G (¾ CUP) SUGAR

NOTE
If you have any leftovers, shred the pork belly, mix it with a bit of the sauce, put some cheese over it and make a really good crusty-bread sandwich.

Who doesn't like slow-cooked, soft pork belly? And if, to something this scrumptious, you add the Mojo Dulce sauce that hundreds of customers in my tapas bars have asked me to bottle and sell, then I think we have a winner.

Preheat the oven to 160°C/325°F/gas mark 3.

Score the skin of the pork belly by running a sharp knife from side to side. Place in a roasting dish, skin side up, rub with the rock salt and pour the wine or beer around the meat. Slow-cook for 4 hours. Add the new potatoes around the meat in the dish 1½ hours before the end of the cooking time.

To make the Mojo Dulce sauce, first measure all the spices, the oregano and the salt into a small bowl. Measure out the sherry vinegar, olive oil and 200ml (¾ cup) water.

Pour another 50ml (3½ Tbsp) water into a small saucepan over a medium heat and add the sugar. Allow the sugar to melt, without stirring, to make a syrup. When the syrup turns to amber, tip in all the dried spices and give them a good stir for about 10 seconds. The caramel will toast the spices very quickly so don't leave them any longer. Pour the vinegar, oil and water mixture straight into the pan and keep stirring so that the caramel dissolves. Simmer over a low heat for 10 minutes and then take a hand blender, while the pan is still over the heat, and blitz for 1 minute to emulsify the sauce. Keep the blender away from the heat source.

Serve your pork belly with the roasted new potatoes and pour the thick Mojo Dulce over the top.

See photographs on following pages.

★ CHORIZO AL VINO ★

CHORIZO COOKED IN WINE

SERVES 6 AS A TAPA

4 FRESH CHORIZO SAUSAGES

175ML (¾ CUP) WHITE WINE

1 TSP SOFT BROWN SUGAR

1 BAY LEAF

BREAD, TO SERVE

Add chorizo to any dish and it will be transformed into something really tasty. In this case chorizo is the main event, so prepare yourself for an explosion of flavour. All you need is just three ingredients and a pan and you'll have a great tapa to surprise your guests with.

Place the whole sausages in a pan together with the wine, sugar and bay leaf. Cook over a high heat for about 15 minutes. The wine should eventually reduce down to a rich syrup.

Remove the sausages from the sauce and cut them into thick slices. Serve as a tapa with some bread to dip in the sauce.

See photograph on page 34.

★ HIGADITOS AL JEREZ DULCE ★

CHICKEN LIVERS WITH SWEET SHERRY WINE AND SPICES

SERVES 2

200G (7OZ) CHICKEN LIVERS

1 TSP SWEET PIMENTÓN
(SWEET SMOKED PAPRIKA)

1 TSP GROUND CUMIN

1 TBSP PLAIN (ALL-PURPOSE) FLOUR

50ML (3½ TBSP) OLIVE OIL

3 GARLIC CLOVES, SKIN ON

3 SPRIGS FRESH THYME

1 TBSP HONEY

2 TBSP SWEET SHERRY WINE,
SUCH AS PEDRO XIMENEZ

SALT

TOAST OR CREAMY MASHED POTATO,
TO SERVE

Chicken livers are so good when prepared as a pâté, and yet so difficult to make tasty when cooked by other methods. This, however, is the type of recipe that will have you licking your fingers for all its sticky sweetness.

Rub the chicken livers with the sweet pimentón and cumin, season with a bit of salt and coat them evenly in the flour.

Pour the olive oil into a large frying pan over a high heat and when it starts to smoke add the garlic cloves and chicken livers, cooking for about 2 minutes on each side. Be careful as the oil will spit.

Add the fresh thyme and honey and flambé with the sweet sherry wine. To do this, slowly tilt the pan towards the flame until the sherry catches, or light with a match. Let the flames flare up then die down, then sauté for 30 seconds so that the chicken livers are fully coated with the sweet honey and sherry. Serve over toast or creamy mashed potato.

★ CANELONES TRUFADOS ★

CANNELLONI WITH TRUFFLES

SERVES 4

EXTRA VIRGIN OLIVE OIL, FOR FRYING

2 SMALL ONIONS, FINELY CHOPPED

500G (1LB 2OZ) MINCED (GROUND) PORK
(ASK YOUR BUTCHER IF THEY CAN USE THE MEAT FROM THE COLLAR)

1 ROASTED CHICKEN BREAST, SHREDDED

100G (3½OZ) SERRANO HAM, CUT INTO SMALL STRIPS

1 BAY LEAF

5 SPRIGS FRESH THYME

1 LARGE APPLE, PEELED AND CUT INTO SMALL CHUNKS

A GENEROUS DRIZZLE OF SWEET SHERRY WINE

200G (¾ CUP) TINNED CHOPPED TOMATOES

12 DRIED CANNELLONI PASTA TUBES

10G (⅓OZ) TRUFFLE

10G (2 TBSP) GRATED CHEDDAR

SALT AND FRESHLY GROUND BLACK PEPPER

FOR THE BÉCHAMEL

100G (7 TBSP) BUTTER

150G (1 CUP + 2 TBSP) PLAIN (ALL-PURPOSE) FLOUR

1 TSP SALT

A PINCH OF GRATED NUTMEG

A PINCH OF GROUND WHITE PEPPER

600ML (2½ CUPS) MILK

Catalonian mothers are real professionals when it comes to making *canelones*, which is a dish traditionally made with the leftovers from the Catalonian *escudella* stew. They can be filled with many different things – however this recipe, stuffed with pork meat, apple and truffle, is the best combination ever.

Start by preparing the béchamel. Melt the butter in a small pan over a high heat and add the flour. Stir for 5 minutes to toast the flour, then add the salt, nutmeg and white pepper and pour in the milk, a little at a time, stirring constantly. Reduce the heat to the lowest it will go and simmer for 10 minutes. If your béchamel is thicker than honey, add a bit more milk to loosen it.

Pour a generous drizzle of olive oil into a frying pan and place over a medium heat. Add the onions and cook for about 4 minutes, until soft and transparent. Add the pork, chicken, Serrano ham, bay leaf, thyme, salt and pepper. Mix all the ingredients well and make sure the meat is loose. Cook for 5 minutes before adding the apple and sherry wine, then cook for a further 3 minutes and add the chopped tomatoes. Simmer for about 15 minutes, stirring from time to time. Add 4 tablespoons of the béchamel and set aside to cool.

Preheat the oven to 180°C/350°F/gas mark 4.

Cover the base of an oven dish with some of the béchamel sauce. Using your hands, stuff the cannelloni tubes with the mince mixture and lay them in the oven dish. Grate the truffle straight into the white sauce, stir and then pour it all over the pasta. Top with the grated cheese and bake for about 20 minutes, until the cheese is nicely browned, then serve.

★ CACHOPO ASTURIANO ★

SPANISH CORDON BLEU

SERVES 4

4 TBSP PLAIN (ALL-PURPOSE) FLOUR

100G (2 CUPS) BREADCRUMBS

2 EGGS, BEATEN

4 RUMP (SIRLOIN) STEAKS, FAT REMOVED

4 SLICES SMOKED HAM

4 SLICES CHEDDAR

4 SLICES SERRANO HAM

SALT AND FRESHLY GROUND BLACK PEPPER

OLIVE OIL, FOR FRYING

It may sound ridiculous, but this has been the most on-trend dish for the last few years back in Spain. So, if you travel there, and not just in Asturias – I mean anywhere across the peninsula – order one. It is in essence a 'cordon bleu' – a fried, breadcrumbed steak wrapped in ham and cheese. As messy as it sounds, believe me, it's worth the fuss!

Spread out the flour on one plate, the breadcrumbs on another and tip the beaten eggs into a shallow bowl.

Use a meat tenderizer or rolling pin to flatten the steaks as thinly as possible without breaking them.

Take one of the flattened steaks and lay a slice of the smoked ham over one half. Lay a slice of cheddar on top and then a slice of the Serrano ham. Sprinkle with salt and freshly ground black pepper. Wrap the steak over the filling like you're closing a book. Repeat until all of the steaks are filled.

Take one steak and coat it first in flour, then egg and finally breadcrumbs. Repeat with the rest of the steaks.

Heat some oil in a wide frying pan set over a medium heat. When the oil is hot, add the steaks to the pan and fry for 2 minutes on each side until perfectly golden. Drain any excess oil and enjoy while hot.

See photographs on following pages.

★ ALBONDIGAS A LA TRUFA ★

MEATBALLS IN BLACK TRUFFLE SAUCE

SERVES 4

2 SLICES WHITE BREAD (CRUSTS REMOVED), BROKEN INTO PIECES

140ML (SCANT ⅔ CUP) WHOLE MILK

500G (2¼ CUPS) FINELY MINCED (GROUND) BEEF (OR A MIXTURE OF MEATS, SUCH AS PORK, CHICKEN OR TURKEY)

100G (½ CUP) MEAT PÂTÉ

SALT AND FRESHLY GROUND BLACK PEPPER

PLAIN (ALL-PURPOSE) FLOUR, FOR DUSTING

OLIVE OIL, FOR FRYING

FOR THE BLACK TRUFFLE SAUCE

25G (1 TBSP + 2 TSP) BUTTER

A DRIZZLE OF OLIVE OIL

1 BUNCH SPRING ONIONS (SCALLIONS), FINELY CHOPPED

1 CARROT, FINELY CHOPPED

75G (1 HEAPED CUP) BUTTON OR OYSTER MUSHROOMS, FINELY CHOPPED

25G (3½ TBSP) PLAIN (ALL-PURPOSE) FLOUR

60ML (¼ CUP) WHITE WINE

½ LITRE (2 CUPS) BEEF, CHICKEN OR VEGETABLE STOCK

1 TSP SALT

1 TSP FINELY CHOPPED ROSEMARY

100ML (½ CUP) DOUBLE (HEAVY) CREAM

2 BLACK TRUFFLES

Truffles are delicate in flavour and aroma. Spain is one of the biggest producers of black truffles in Europe, supplying top restaurants all over the world. You can get them in brine in supermarkets these days, which is handy.

Place the bread in a bowl and pour over the milk. Set aside to soak.

In a separate bowl, mix together the meat and the pâté. Add the soaked bread and season with salt and freshly ground black pepper. Mix until smooth and well combined. Form meatballs by rolling walnut-sized pieces of the mixture between your hands. They should be about 30g (1oz) each. Dust the meatballs in flour.

Heat some oil in a shallow pan over a medium-high heat and fry the meatballs just until they are golden. Do not overcook at this stage as we are going to finish them in the sauce. Set aside.

To make the sauce, heat the butter and olive oil in a pan over a medium-low heat and add the finely chopped spring onions, carrot and mushrooms. Cook for about 10 minutes, until the onion is transparent. Reduce the temperature to low and add the flour to the pan, stirring with a wooden spoon to make a roux. Cook for about 4 minutes and then add the wine, continuing to stir until you get a paste and the alcohol has evaporated, then add the stock with the salt and rosemary. Keep stirring and cooking until the sauce thickens, then add the cream, stirring so that the mixture doesn't split or curdle. Add the meatballs to the sauce and cook for a further 5 minutes.

Grate the truffles into the sauce and serve immediately as the truffles lose their aroma quickly.

★ CONEJO EN SALMOREJO ★

RABBIT WITH A CANARY ISLANDS SAUCE

SERVES 4

200ML (¾ CUP) WHITE WINE

A DRIZZLE OF EXTRA VIRGIN OLIVE OIL

1 TBSP DRIED OREGANO

4 GARLIC CLOVES, CHOPPED

1 TBSP SWEET PIMENTÓN
(SWEET SMOKED PAPRIKA)

1 SMALL DRIED CHILLI PEPPER,
CHOPPED

1 WHOLE RABBIT, CUT INTO 8 PIECES

1 BAY LEAF

5 SPRIGS FRESH THYME

OLIVE OIL, FOR FRYING

400ML (1¾ CUPS) CHICKEN STOCK

ROCK OR SEA SALT AND FRESHLY
GROUND BLACK PEPPER

This dish is from our beloved Canary Islands.
We call them the fortunate islands because the
sun is always shining down there. The tricky bit
of this recipe is to get the right *salmorejo* sauce
to marinate the rabbit, not to be confused with
the tomato, bread and oil *salmorejo* typical of
Córdoba in southern Spain.

In a bowl or food processor, blend together
2 tablespoons of the white wine, a drizzle of extra
virgin olive oil, the oregano, chopped garlic, sweet
pimentón and the chopped chilli. Rub this marinade
over the pieces of rabbit, add the bay leaf and thyme
and refrigerate overnight if you have the time,
otherwise never mind.

Heat a good drizzle of olive oil in a frying pan over a
high heat. Remove the excess marinade from the rabbit
(keep it for later), sprinkle with salt and pan-fry the
pieces for about 3 minutes on each side, or until
browned. Season with salt and pepper.

Add the leftover marinade to the pan, including
the bay leaf and thyme, and fry for a further 4 minutes.
Add the remaining white wine and allow to reduce
down completely before adding the chicken stock.
Simmer all together for 10 minutes, shaking the
pan now and then to form a rich, intense sauce.

MORCILLA DE BURGOS ★ CON MANZANA ★

SPANISH RICE BLACK PUDDING WITH CARAMELIZED APPLE

SERVES 4 AS A TAPA

1 X LARGE MORCILLA DE BURGOS
(SPANISH RICE BLACK PUDDING)

1 CINNAMON STICK

2 APPLES, ANY VARIETY,
SEEDED AND CUT INTO WEDGES

1 TBSP PINE NUTS

1 TBSP HONEY

A PINCH OF SEA SALT

OLIVE OIL, FOR FRYING

BREAD, TO SERVE

I have a weakness for black pudding (and offal in general). To me, it's a total delicacy, so good that I don't like to eat it too often otherwise it stops being special. I do the same with jamón ibérico. In this dish the apple and honey are the perfect match for the main event.

Cut the black pudding into finger-width slices and set aside.

Add the cinnamon stick to a frying pan over a medium heat. Add the apple wedges and cook for at least 3 minutes on each side, adding the pine nuts to the pan for the last 3 minutes. Drizzle the honey into the pan and continue to cook until the apples are lightly caramelized. Season with a pinch of salt.

Heat a generous drizzle of olive oil in a separate pan over a high heat and cook the black pudding slices for 2 minutes on each side so that the edges are crispy.

Serve together on a plate and enjoy with lots of good bread.

ESTOFADO DE CORZO
★ CON SETAS ★

VENISON AND WILD MUSHROOM STEW WITH OLIVE OIL MASH
(MY FAMILY STYLE)

SERVES 6

2KG (4½LB) SHOULDER OF VENISON

1 X 75CL BOTTLE SPANISH RED WINE

OLIVE OIL, FOR FRYING

1 CARROT, ROUGHLY CHOPPED

1 CELERY STICK, ROUGHLY CHOPPED

1 ONION, ROUGHLY CHOPPED

2 TOMATOES, CHOPPED

2 BAY LEAVES

1 SPRIG FRESH THYME

1 SPRIG FRESH ROSEMARY

1 SPRIG FRESH MARJORAM

5 BLACK PEPPERCORNS

2 CLOVES

½ CINNAMON STICK

25ML (1 TBSP + 2 TSP) BRANDY

500G (1LB 2OZ) WILD MUSHROOMS

570ML (2¼ CUPS) BEEF STOCK

SALT

FOR THE MASHED POTATOES

1KG (2LB 3OZ) WAXY POTATOES

200G (¾ CUP + 2 TBSP) BUTTER

100ML (⅓ CUP + 1 TBSP) OLIVE OIL

100ML (½ CUP) DOUBLE
(HEAVY) CREAM

SALT AND FRESHLY GROUND
BLACK PEPPER

In autumn and winter my uncles and cousins would go hunting in the mountains of Madrid, but not all of us liked hunting, so we used to pick mushrooms along the way. This was a dish that would be on the table a couple of days later, after we'd chopped up and marinated the animal.

Cut the venison into big chunks and leave to marinate overnight in the red wine.

The next day, drain the wine and reserve it for later. Heat some olive oil in a deep pan or roasting tray over a high heat and fry the venison pieces to seal them. Remove and set aside. If you plan to slow-cook the stew in the oven, preheat it to 160°C/325°F/gas mark 3.

Add a little more oil to the pan and add the carrot, celery and onion. Cook for 20 minutes until caramelized and then add the tomatoes, herbs and spices. Return the meat to the pan and pour over the brandy and reserved wine. Cook until reduced by half.

Add the wild mushrooms and the beef stock and season with a little salt. Bring to the boil and then cover. Slow-cook the stew either over a low heat or in the oven for at least 3 hours, until the meat falls apart and you have an unctuous and rich sauce. Leave the oven on.

To make the mashed potatoes, peel, wash and cut the potatoes into even slices and place them in a large pan. Cover with cold water and bring to the boil over a high heat. Cook for about 15 minutes until soft, drain and return to the same pan. Set over a low heat for 1 minute to dry. Add the butter, salt and pepper and start mashing using a whisk. Add the olive oil and cream and mix. Tip onto a baking sheet and bake on the top shelf of the oven for 20 minutes so that it crisps up and lightly browns. Serve hot with the venison stew.

PESCADOS Y MARISCOS

FISH & SEAFOOD

★ MERLUZA A LA GALLEGA ★

GALICIAN-STYLE HAKE

SERVES 4

2 MEDIUM ONIONS, PEELED
AND HALVED

1 TBSP SALT, PLUS EXTRA
FOR SEASONING

1 BAY LEAF

4 MEDIUM WHITE POTATOES, HALVED

4 HAKE SUPREMES OR FILLETS

100ML (⅓ CUP) OLIVE OIL

4 GARLIC CLOVES, SLICED

1 TSP SWEET PIMENTÓN
(SWEET SMOKED PAPRIKA)

FRESHLY GROUND BLACK PEPPER

A dish with soft, subtle flavours – nothing punchy – that is all good and healthy. Sometimes comfort is found in the most basic form of cooking. Call me crazy but I find this dish sublime.

Place a large deep pan over a high heat. Add 850ml (3½ cups) water, the onions, and bay leaf. Bring to the boil, add the potatoes and cook for about 13 minutes until they are half cooked.

Season the hake with salt and pepper and add it to the water with the potatoes, making sure they are completely covered by water and adding more if necessary. Cook for another 6 minutes and then remove from the heat. Carefully remove the delicate fish and potatoes from the pan, keeping the fish whole. Set aside 150ml (⅔ cup) of the cooking liquid.

Meanwhile, heat the olive oil in a small frying pan and cook the garlic until golden. Add the pimentón along with the reserved cooking liquid and boil for about 1 minute.

Serve 2 potato halves, half an onion and a portion of fish per plate with a little of the garlic and pimentón sauce poured over the top.

PARGO CON CALABACIN, ★ ESPINACA Y ACEITUNAS ★

RED SNAPPER WITH COURGETTE, OLIVES AND SPINACH

SERVES 4

2 X 500-G (1LB-2OZ) RED SNAPPERS
(OR ANY OTHER FISH)

4 TBSP OLIVE OIL, PLUS A DRIZZLE

2 PINCHES OF ROCK OR SEA SALT

4 GARLIC CLOVES, THINLY SLICED

A HANDFUL PITTED BLACK
OLIVES, HALVED

1 COURGETTE (ZUCCHINI),
ABOUT 200G (7OZ), DICED

1 TSP SWEET PIMENTÓN
(SWEET SMOKED PAPRIKA)

A HANDFUL FROZEN PEAS,
DEFROSTED

3 TBSP SHERRY VINEGAR

100G (2 CUPS) BABY SPINACH

2 TBSP FINELY CHOPPED
FRESH CHIVES

SALT AND FRESHLY GROUND
BLACK PEPPER

I eat this for dinner at least once a month. It's easy to make, with ingredients you can find in any supermarket, and it's quick and healthy! And, let's face it, I love fish above anything else.

Ask your fishmonger to gut and scale your fish. At home just wash them in cold water and pat them dry really well with a cloth or kitchen paper.

Place a pan wide enough to hold the entire fish over a medium heat. Drizzle over some olive oil, season both sides of the fish with the salt and pan-fry for about 5 minutes on each side, until crispy and fully cooked. If you put a lid over the pan it will create an oven so that the fish cooks all over and not just on the sides in contact with the pan. Just leave a little opening so that the steam can escape and doesn't condensate on the lid and fall back into the pan, stopping the fish from crisping up properly.

Meanwhile, heat the 4 tablespoons oil in a large frying pan over a high heat. Add the garlic and cook until starting to turn golden, then add the olives and cook for 30 seconds before adding the diced courgette. Fry for 1 minute and then add the sweet pimentón and the peas. Give the pan a good stir and, after 30 seconds, pour over the sherry vinegar and let it reduce for a few seconds. Add the baby spinach and season with salt and pepper, then add the finely chopped chives.

Serve the fish whole with the vegetables alongside.

BACALAO Y GAMBAS
★ AL AZAFRAN CON QUINOA ★

COD, PRAWNS AND QUINOA WITH SAFFRON SAUCE

SERVES 4

16 WHOLE LARGE PRAWNS

OLIVE OIL, FOR FRYING

½ ONION, THINLY SLICED

½ LEEK, THINLY SLICED

4 GARLIC CLOVES, THINLY SLICED

1G (2 TSP) SAFFRON THREADS

1 TSP SWEET PIMENTÓN
(SWEET SMOKED PAPRIKA)

1 TBSP TOMATO PURÉE (PASTE)

25ML (1 TBSP + 2 TSP) BRANDY

100ML (⅓ CUP + 1 TBSP) WHITE WINE

200G (7OZ) QUINOA, RINSED

200ML (¾ CUP) SINGLE (LIGHT) CREAM

4 X 150-G (5¼-OZ) COD LOINS

SALT AND GROUND WHITE PEPPER

Every time I use the head and shells of prawns to make a shellfish stock for a dish, I know that the end result is going to have a refined taste, whether it's a seafood paella or a fish stew.

Peel the prawns and keep the heads and shells for the stock. Set aside the tails. Pour a small drizzle of olive oil into a medium pan over a high heat and fry the heads and shells of the prawns for 5 minutes until golden, stirring constantly so that they cook on all sides, and then pour in 1 litre (5 cups) water. Bring to the boil and cook for 20 minutes, then blend with a hand blender for 20 seconds to squeeze as much flavour from the heads as possible. Pass through a fine sieve and set aside.

Pour 5 tablespoons oil into a large frying pan over a medium heat and sweat the onion and leek for 15 minutes. Add the garlic and fry over a high heat for 3 minutes, then add the saffron, sweet pimentón and tomato purée. Cook for 2 minutes, then flambé with the brandy followed by the white wine. To do this, slowly tilt the pan towards the flame until the brandy catches, or light with a match. Let the flames flare up then die down.

Add the quinoa to the pan, season and pour over the reserved prawn stock. Cook over a low heat for about 20 minutes, or until the quinoa is tender. Add the cream and prawns, stir and bring back to the boil. Cook for 3 minutes, taking care not to overcook the prawns. Meanwhile, pour a little olive oil into a separate pan over a high heat. Season the cod and fry, skin side down, until cooked – 5–10 minutes depending on the thickness. If really thick, carefully turn them over after 5 minutes so that they cook on both sides.

Lay a bed of saffron quinoa on each plate and top with the cod loins.

★ ATUN CON TOMATE ★

TUNA IN TOMATO SAUCE

SERVES 4

4 TBSP OLIVE OIL

1 LARGE ONION, DICED

1 GREEN ROMANO OR BELL PEPPER, SLICED

4 GARLIC CLOVES, CHOPPED

1 TSP SWEET PIMENTÓN (SWEET SMOKED PAPRIKA)

500G (1LB 2OZ) CHOPPED PEELED TOMATOES (TINNED IS FINE)

1 TSP DEMERARA SUGAR

½ TSP DRIED OREGANO OR 2 SPRIGS FRESH OREGANO

1 BAY LEAF

4 X 150-G (5¼-OZ) TUNA LOIN STEAKS

SALT AND GROUND WHITE PEPPER

This is one of the recipes my mother cooks at home all the time. She makes a very tasty sauce but, with all respect to my mum, she overcooks the fish in a very old-fashioned way. I don't blame her, that is just how she learned to cook it! This is my fresher and lighter version of this home classic, which I will cook for her soon; let's see what she thinks.

Heat the olive oil in a large saucepan over a medium heat and add the onion, pepper and garlic. Fry for 15 minutes, until the onion is soft and transparent. Add the sweet pimentón and stir for 15 seconds before adding the tomatoes, sugar, oregano, bay leaf and a little black pepper. The sugar will reduce the acidity of the tomato, making a more pleasant sauce. I personally like a sweeter tomato sauce, but that's just me! Cook over a medium heat for at least 20 minutes, until the sauce has reduced a bit and has a rich consistency.

Cut each tuna steak into 6 pieces, season with a bit of salt and add the pieces to the tomato sauce. Simmer for 3 minutes and serve while the tuna is still pink in the middle.

★ CARPACCIO DE ATUN ★

TUNA CARPACCIO WITH OLIVE, MANGO AND CAPER DRESSING

SERVES 4

300G (10½OZ) FRESH TUNA LOIN, ABOUT 4CM (1½IN) WIDE AND 20CM (8IN) LONG

1 LEMON

½ MANGO, PEELED AND DICED SMALL

6 PITTED BLACK OLIVES, HALVED

1 FRESH RED CHILLI PEPPER, FINELY CHOPPED

1 TBSP FINELY CHOPPED FRESH CHIVES

2 TBSP CAPERS

6 TBSP EXTRA VIRGIN OLIVE OIL

A FEW FRESH CORIANDER (CILANTRO) LEAVES

A PINCH OF SEA SALT

In Spain we fish tuna off both the north and south coasts of the peninsula. It is very highly regarded, a real delicacy that's pricey but worth every penny. Whether preserved in a glass jar, stewed or served raw, its particular taste and texture transform any recipe into a treat. On a hot summer's day, this lean dish will bring you a smile.

Cut the tuna into 2 smaller loins about 4cm (1½ in) wide and 10cm (4in) long and sear very lightly on all sides in a very hot, dry pan, for about 10 seconds on each side. Wrap in plastic wrap and freeze for 2 hours.

Remove the plastic wrap from the chilled tuna and cut into 5-mm (¼-in) slices with a sharp knife. Arrange on a plate.

Zest the lemon and then remove the peel and cut the flesh into small cubes. Place in a bowl with the mango, olives, chilli pepper and chives. Add the capers and olive oil, mix well and then use to dress the tuna. Garnish with the coriander, season with a bit of salt and enjoy.

★ MERLUZA A LA ROMANA ★

HAKE A LA ROMANA WITH MAYONNAISE

SERVES 2 AS A MAIN OR 4 AS A TAPA

100ML (⅓ CUP) OLIVE OIL

100ML (½ CUP) SUNFLOWER OIL

100G (¾ CUP) PLAIN
(ALL-PURPOSE) FLOUR

1 EGG, BEATEN

2 SKINLESS HAKE SUPREMES,
EACH WEIGHING ABOUT 175G (6¼OZ)

SALT

LEMON WEDGES AND GRATED ZEST,
TO SERVE

MAYONNAISE (SEE PAGE 26), TO SERVE

NOTE
After you have finished frying the fish, pour the leftover egg (which will have bits of flour in it) into the hot oil and fry it. We call this 'huevo tonto', which translates literally as 'silly egg'.

'A la romana' is how we define our batter, which is traditionally used for fish but is also used to coat squid or chicken. So, as in England, we also coat fish and fry it, however our batter is lighter, as you will see in this recipe. I have a feeling this is the most used technique for cooking fish all over Spain. Every mother of every friend I know cooks fish this way and mine does too. It's as easy as it gets. It is a delicious way to prepare fish because it gets perfectly cooked inside and is not at all heavy, unless you use fries as a garnish! The mayonnaise is just the perfect match.

Mix the oils together in a frying pan and place over a medium heat. The oil should not be too hot or it will burn the batter.

Spread out the flour on a plate. Tip the beaten egg into a shallow bowl.

Season the fish with a little salt. If you are going to serve it as a tapa, cut it into bite-sized pieces or goujons. Coat the pieces in the flour, shake off the excess and immediately place it in the beaten egg to coat it well. Shake again to remove the excess and submerge in the hot oil. The oil should sizzle gently. Cook for 5 minutes and then turn the fish and cook for another 3 minutes or so, depending on the size, until golden. Set aside on kitchen paper to drain the excess oil.

Serve with the lemon wedges, Mayonnaise and a sprinkling of lemon zest alongside a fresh salad; try any one from the salad chapter in this book!

★ RAPE A LA DONOSTIARRA ★

MONKFISH WITH FRIED GARLIC AND PAPRIKA

SERVES 2

1 LARGE ONION, SLICED INTO
5-MM (¼-IN) RINGS

1 LARGE ROASTING POTATO,
PEELED AND CUT INTO
3-MM (⅛-IN) SLICES

100ML (⅓ CUP) EXTRA VIRGIN OLIVE
OIL

1 MONKFISH TAIL, ABOUT 1KG (2LB 3OZ)
OR 2 X 500-G (1LB-2OZ) TAILS, CLEANED

5 GARLIC CLOVES, SLICED

1 CAYENNE CHILLI PEPPER

1 TSP SWEET PIMENTÓN
(SWEET SMOKED PAPRIKA)

A DRIZZLE OF WHITE VINEGAR

SALT AND FRESHLY GROUND
BLACK PEPPER

Donostia is the Basque name for San Sebastián in northern Spain. The culinary culture there is quite extraordinary and very rich, not only for their famous *pintxos* but also for traditional dishes such as this one. The Basque region has brought us the best Spanish chefs, restaurants and a whole range of innovative cooking techniques. This fish dish, though, is as traditional as it gets.

Preheat the oven to 180°C/350°F/gas mark 4 and line a roasting tray with parchment paper or foil.

Lay the onion rings over the tray to make a bed for the fish. Lay the potato slices on top and season with a pinch of salt and a drizzle of the oil. Bake for about 25 minutes, then take the tray out of the oven and lay the fish on top of the potato. Drizzle with more oil and season with salt and pepper. Cook for a further 15 minutes, or until the fish is cooked through.

Meanwhile, place a small saucepan over a medium heat with the remaining oil and cook the garlic slices and cayenne pepper until they start to turn golden. Add the sweet pimentón followed by the vinegar and mix well, being careful at this stage because the vinegar can splash out of the pan.

Serve the monkfish over the onions and potatoes with the sauce poured over the top.

★ OSTRAS EN SALSA VERDE ★

OYSTERS COOKED IN SALSA VERDE

SERVES 2

6 OYSTERS

2 TBSP OLIVE OIL

1 GARLIC CLOVE, FINELY CHOPPED

1 TBSP FINELY CHOPPED
FLAT-LEAF PARSLEY

1 TSP PLAIN (ALL-PURPOSE) FLOUR

25ML (1 TBSP + 2 TSP) WHITE WINE

140ML (SCANT ⅔ CUP) WATER

SALT AND FRESHLY GROUND
BLACK PEPPER

Oysters might be seen as a luxury ingredient but I have found them as cheap as 50p (under a dollar) a shell and, if you think about it, an oyster has at least four times the meat of most clams. I think the maths work, if you know what I mean. The texture of the slow-cooked oysters in this sauce is just delicious.

Open the oysters and remove the meat. Place the open shells over rock salt on a nice-looking plate for later.

In a small saucepan, heat the oil with the garlic and fry until light golden. Add the finely chopped parsley, flour and some seasoning and stir for 1 minute. Add the wine and water and stir in the oyster meat with the juices. Cook for 1 minute and then spoon into the open oyster shells and serve.

★ TXANGURRO AL CAVA ★

BAKED CRAB WITH CAVA

SERVES 4 AS A STARTER

1KG (2LB 3OZ) LIVE BROWN
OR SPIDER CRAB

3 TBSP OLIVE OIL

2 GARLIC CLOVES, CHOPPED

½ ONION, CHOPPED

1 SMALL TOMATO, CHOPPED

60ML (¼ CUP) CAVA

1 TBSP COARSE BREADCRUMBS

25ML (1 TBSP + 2 TSP) BRANDY

SALT AND FRESHLY GROUND
BLACK PEPPER

At Christmas in Spain it's all about shellfish, good ham and big centrepieces like suckling pig, milk-fed lambs and turkeys. We have this crab dish as a starter on 24th December every single year.

Place the crab in the freezer for 2 hours before cooking it. This will sedate it and make for a more humane death when it is cooked.

Bring a large pan of salted water to the boil and boil the crab for 15 minutes. Allow to cool a little and then pull off the claws and pick all the meat from them. Open the top shell where the claws were attached to the body by pulling it apart from the main shell and spoon out the meat. You may need to cut the inner shell into a few pieces to access all the meat. Keep the main shell for presentation.

Preheat the oven to 200°C/400°F/gas mark 6.

Heat the oil in a frying pan over a medium heat and cook the garlic and onion until translucent, about 10 minutes. Add the crab meat and sauté for 2 minutes, then add the tomato and the cava. Season with salt and pepper.

Fill the crab shell with the crab mixture, top with the breadcrumbs and bake for 10 minutes.

Heat the brandy in a saucepan over a medium heat just until you start to see bubbles rising. Pour the hot brandy over the breadcrumbs and quickly flambé at the table by lighting the alcohol with a long match. Make sure you do this slightly away from your guests and away from anything flammable, and check that no alcohol has splashed onto the tablecloth before you light it. Serve as soon as the flames die down.

★ BERBERECHOS AL FINO ★

COCKLES IN A DRY SHERRY SAUCE

SERVES 2

4 TBSP EXTRA VIRGIN OLIVE OIL

2 GARLIC CLOVES, FINELY CHOPPED

1 CAYENNE CHILLI PEPPER,
FINELY CHOPPED

1 SLICE SERRANO HAM,
FINELY CHOPPED

200G (7OZ) COCKLES, CLEANED
AND ANY OPEN OR DAMAGED
SHELLS DISCARDED

25ML (1 TBSP + 2 TSP) FINO SHERRY

2 TBSP FINELY CHOPPED
FRESH PARSLEY

SALT AND FRESHLY GROUND
BLACK PEPPER

In Spain, anything with two shells we just love, as long as it comes with a lovely sauce we can mop up with bread when the plate is finished.

Pour the olive oil into a small frying pan over a high heat and fry the finely chopped garlic, chilli and Serrano ham until golden.

Add the cockles to the pan, season with salt and pepper and pour over the Fino sherry. Cover and let the cockles steam for about 2 minutes.

Sprinkle with the finely chopped parsley and serve.

NOTE
This dish works equally well with any other shellfish, such as mussels or clams. Use what is in season and at its best.

★ ALMEJAS A LA MARINERA ★

CLAMS FISHERMAN-STYLE

SERVES 4 AS A TAPA

600G (1LB 5OZ) CLAMS, CLEANED
AND ANY OPEN OR DAMAGED
SHELLS DISCARDED

60ML (¼ CUP) EXTRA VIRGIN
OLIVE OIL

½ ONION, FINELY CHOPPED

2 GARLIC CLOVES, FINELY CHOPPED

¼ RED CHILLI PEPPER,
FINELY CHOPPED

2 TSP PLAIN (ALL-PURPOSE) FLOUR

1 TSP SWEET PIMENTÓN
(SWEET SMOKED PAPRIKA)

1 TSP SALT

160ML (⅔ CUP) WHITE WINE

2 TBSP FINELY CHOPPED
FRESH PARSLEY

This dish relies on fresh clams and little more as this is how fishermen would cook them while out on the boat. But it's just as popular on land!

Put the clams in a large bowl or in the sink, cover with cold salty water and leave for 1 hour, moving them around with your hand from time to time. This will help the clams to open and release any sand.

Place a large frying pan over a high heat and add the oil, onion, garlic and chilli and cook until the onion is transparent and soft, about 10 minutes. Reduce the heat and add the flour, pimentón and salt, stirring continuously for 1 minute to cook the flour and make a roux.

Add the wine, little by little, stirring vigorously until the wine and flour are completely combined. Continue to cook for at least 2 minutes over a low heat. If you see that the sauce is getting too thick, add a bit of water. Drain the clams and add them to the pan with the parsley, stir thoroughly, cover and cook for another 2 minutes.

Remove the lid and toss the mixture a few times. By now, all the clams should be open; if not, cover and cook for another minute or so. Discard any clams that do not open before serving.

★ MEJILLONES TIGRE ★

MUSSEL CROQUETTES ON THE SHELL

SERVES 6

50ML (3½ TBSP) WHITE WINE

1 BAY LEAF

1KG (2LB 3OZ) MUSSELS, CLEANED AND ANY OPEN OR DAMAGED SHELLS DISCARDED

50G (3½ TBSP) BUTTER

8 SPRING ONIONS (SCALLIONS), FINELY CHOPPED

1 DRIED CAYENNE CHILLI PEPPER

800ML (3¼ CUPS + 3½ TBSP) WHOLE MILK

110G (¾ CUP + 1½ TBSP) PLAIN (ALL-PURPOSE) FLOUR

1 TEASPOON SALT

A PINCH OF GRATED NUTMEG

A PINCH OF GROUND WHITE PEPPER

2 EGGS

100G (2 CUPS) DRIED BREADCRUMBS

SEA OR ROCK SALT FLAKES

SUNFLOWER OIL, FOR DEEP FRYING

When it comes to great recipes, some are simple while others are a bit more labour intensive, but worth it! This is one of my top 10 favourite tapas recipes. A shellfish béchamel croquette, seafood flavours, creamy texture inside, crispy bite on the surface... you know what I mean.

Put the wine and bay leaf into a deep pan over a high heat and bring to the boil. Add the clean mussels to the pan, cover and cook for about 3 minutes, until they open. Use a slotted spoon to remove the mussels from the pan, retaining the cooking liquid. Set aside the mussels to cool, retaining the juices released from the shells. Once warm, separate the meat from the shells and remove any filaments as you will be using the shells for serving later. Finely chop the meat and set aside.

Melt the butter in a pan over a medium heat and add the spring onions and cayenne pepper (yes, someone will end up eating this without realizing. Surprise!). Cook for a few minutes until the onions turn transparent but not brown.

Meanwhile, pour the milk into a separate pan over a medium-high heat with 100ml (⅓ cup) of the cooking liquid. Bring almost to the boil, then take off the heat and set aside.

Add 60g (scant ½ cup) of the flour to the spring onions and cook for a further 5 minutes, stirring constantly until the flour has toasted a little. Add the hot milk mixture, a ladleful at a time, whisking and stirring constantly until all the liquid is added to the pan and you have a silky smooth white sauce. Bring to the boil and then reduce the heat to low, scraping the bottom of the pan occasionally to stop the sauce

Continued overleaf

Recipe continued

from catching and burning. If you think this has happened and the sauce smells smoky, pour it into a clean pan to continue cooking but avoid scraping up the burnt bits in the bottom of the pan.

After 30 minutes of cooking over a low heat, add the chopped mussels, salt, nutmeg and pepper. Simmer for a further 10 minutes, whisking and stirring from time to time. Taste and season to your liking.

Line a roasting tray with parchment paper and pour the béchamel into it. Spread out the sauce and place a layer of plastic wrap directly over the top to stop a skin forming. Refrigerate for about 2 hours to cool completely and set.

Once the sauce is set well enough to handle, remove the plastic wrap and use a tablespoon to fill the mussel shells with the sauce. Overload them a little bit, don't be shy. They should be set well enough that the sauce doesn't slip out of the shells.

Beat the eggs and tip them into a shallow bowl. Spread out the remaining 50g (6 Tbsp) flour on one plate and the breadcrumbs on another plate. Dip the béchamel side of each shell first into the flour, then the egg and then into the breadcrumbs and set aside on a clean plate. At this point you can chill again in the fridge or even freeze them for future use.

Heat the oil to 180°C/360°F in a large deep pan. Drop the mussels into the hot oil for a couple of minutes until they are golden and crisp. Remove and drain on kitchen paper. It is best to do this in batches so that the oil doesn't cool down too much. Serve sprinkled with sea salt.

MEJILLONES EN VINAGRETA

MUSSELS IN A VEGETABLE AND TOMATO VINAIGRETTE

SERVES 5 AS A TAPA

2 LARGE, RIPE TOMATOES

½ RED ROMANO OR (BELL) PEPPER, FINELY CHOPPED

½ GREEN ROMANO OR (BELL) PEPPER, FINELY CHOPPED

1 SMALL ONION OR A BUNCH OF SPRING ONIONS (SCALLIONS), FINELY CHOPPED

6 TBSP EXTRA VIRGIN OLIVE OIL

3 TBSP SHERRY VINEGAR

1 TSP SALT

250ML (1 CUP) WHITE WINE

1 BAY LEAF

1KG (2LB 3OZ) MUSSELS, CLEANED AND ANY OPEN OR DAMAGED SHELLS DISCARDED

This summery tapas dish is so refreshing and so easy to make that it is almost impossible to fail. These days it can be seen as old fashioned and I don't see it as much as I would like in typical Spanish bars any more. Well, I will be having it on my table every summer, even if it has gone out of fashion!

Cut a cross into the bottom of each tomato with a sharp knife and put them in boiling water for a few seconds. Remove from the water and let cool a little, then peel and cut each one into 4 wedges. Remove the seeds and discard, then cut the tomato flesh into small cubes. This method of preparation is called a tomato concasse.

Mix together the chopped tomatoes, peppers and onion with the oil, sherry vinegar and salt. Set aside.

Make sure your mussels are well cleaned. Use a knife to remove the filaments and any barnacles left on the shells as they will be part of the final presentation.

Put 500ml (2 cups) water and the wine in a deep pan with the bay leaf and bring it to the boil, then add the clean mussels, cover and cook for about 3 minutes, until they open. Remove the mussels from the water and set aside to cool. Add 1 tablespoon of the cooking water to the vinaigrette to enhance the mussel flavour.

Once the mussels have cooled a little, separate the shells and the meat attached and mix this mussel meat with the vinaigrette.

There are many ways to serve this tapa. My favourite is to lay half the shells on a tray and spoon 1 mussel with a bit of sauce into each one. Alternatively, serve over warm buttered toast, gem lettuce leaves... the possibilities are endless.

★ MEJILLONES A LA CREMA ★

MUSSELS IN A CREAM SAUCE

SERVES 10

2 SPRIGS FRESH THYME

1 BAY LEAF

2KG (4½LB) MUSSELS, CLEANED AND ANY OPEN OR DAMAGED SHELLS DISCARDED

OLIVE OIL, FOR FRYING

1 BUNCH SPRING ONIONS (SCALLIONS), FINELY CHOPPED

350ML (1½ CUPS) WHITE WINE

200ML (1½ CUPS) SINGLE (LIGHT) CREAM

1 TBSP CORNFLOUR (CORNSTARCH), OPTIONAL

SALT AND FRESHLY GROUND BLACK PEPPER

NOTE
To minimize splashing when you add the mussels to the hot water, put them in a bowl first and add them to the water in one go.

The mussels we eat in Spain come from the Galician *rias*, cultivated in vast quantities to satisfy Spanish demand. It is also in the north of Spain that you will find most of Spain's dairy products because as well as having wild seas, they have very wet weather that is ideal for cow farming.

Place the thyme and bay leaf in a deep pan with 500ml (2 cups) water, set over a high heat and bring to the boil. Add the mussels, cover and cook for about 3 minutes, until just opened. Remove and set aside, discarding any that haven't opened.

Remove the bay leaf and thyme from the water and boil over a high heat until reduced by half. Set aside.

Pour a drizzle of olive oil into a saucepan over a low heat and fry the onions until soft, about 10 minutes. Add the wine and boil for about 1 minute to make sure all the alcohol has evaporated, then add the reserved cooking water from the mussels. Continue to boil for 6 minutes, then season with salt and pepper and pour in the cream. Reduce the heat to low. If the sauce is too thin, continue to cook for another 6 minutes to reduce it, or dilute the cornflour in cold water and stir it into the sauce.

Add the mussels and mix with the cream sauce to warm them through before serving.

★ CALAMARES EN SU TINTA ★

SQUID IN BLACK INK SAUCE

SERVES 6

1KG (2LB 3OZ) FRESH SQUID OR BABY SQUID, CLEANED (ASK YOUR FISHMONGER TO DO THIS FOR YOU)

6 OR 7 SLICES STALE HARD WHITE BREAD SUCH AS CIABATTA OR BAGUETTE

185ML (¾ CUP) WHITE WINE

6 X 4G SACHETS (1 TBSP + 2 TSP) SQUID INK

5 TBSP OLIVE OIL

3 MEDIUM ONIONS, ROUGHLY CHOPPED

1 SMALL CARROT, ROUGHLY CHOPPED

2 GARLIC CLOVES, FINELY CHOPPED

1 BAY LEAF

200ML (¾ CUP) TOMATO PASSATA (OR STRAINED OR MILLED CANNED TOMATOES)

185ML (¾ CUP) FISH STOCK OR WATER

SALT AND FRESHLY GROUND BLACK PEPPER

Unfortunately, outside the Mediterranean and Asia squid is only popular as fried rings. I sometimes wonder if people believe that squid are actually rings that swim in the sea! In Spain we cook squid in many different ways and it's a fundamental ingredient in so many recipes. In this one it's all about the depth of flavour because to me, if there is a flavour of the sea it is in squid ink. I consider this dish to be a showstopper and it's not just because of the colour!

Cut the squid tubes into rings and set aside with the tentacles. If you have baby squid, stuff the tentacles inside the tubes and close with a toothpick.

Toast the bread and then place it in a mixing bowl with the white wine and the squid ink. Set aside.

Pour the olive oil into a deep pan. Set over a medium heat and add the chopped vegetables, garlic and bay leaf and fry slowly for about 8 minutes or until the onions look transparent. Add the passata, reduce the heat to low and cook for another 2 minutes, stirring continuously with a wooden spoon to stop the sauce from catching.

Add the inky bread and the fish stock, season with salt and pepper and cook over a low heat for another 15 minutes before blending to make a thick, shiny black sauce with reddish hints. If it is too thick you can add some more water or fish stock.

Finally, add the squid to the sauce and cook for 20 minutes, or until the squid is soft.

SEPIA A LA PLANCHA
★ CON AJILIMOJI ★
GRILLED CUTTLEFISH

SERVES 2

1 TBSP CHOPPED FLAT-LEAF PARSLEY

2 GARLIC CLOVES, FINELY CHOPPED

4 TBSP OLIVE OIL, PLUS EXTRA
FOR DRIZZLING

1 CUTTLEFISH (ABOUT 500G [1LB 2OZ]),
CLEANED (ASK YOUR FISHMONGER
TO DO THIS FOR YOU)

1 HEAPED TBSP ROCK OR SEA SALT

2 LEMON WEDGES, TO SERVE

If you ask anyone in Spain for '*sepia a la plancha*', or grilled cuttlefish, it will bring back memories of moments at *chiringuitos*, or beach huts, with family or friends. Instead of having this dish in a fancy restaurant, it's best to have it at a traditional al fresco beach bar. The trick is definitely in the olive oil with the garlic and parsley – I'm sure you will get it right. It couldn't be any easier to make at home.

In a bowl, mix together the parsley, garlic and olive oil.

It is important to prepare the cuttlefish before cooking, otherwise it will be tough and won't cook evenly. Make sure you remove all the layers of skin until there is only white flesh and then, with a sharp knife, score the inside of the body in a cross-hatch pattern.

To cook '*a la plancha*' requires a very hot pan, as hot as it can get. Place a large, dry frying pan over a high heat. While the pan is getting hot, sprinkle the salt over the surface. When you can feel the heat over the pan, place the cuttlefish on top of the salt and drizzle it with a little olive oil.

After 2 minutes, drizzle the cuttlefish with 2 tablespoons of the prepared parsley oil and turn it over. Be aware that it will smoke a lot and this will give the fish a 'plancha-style' aroma. Cook for at least another 2 minutes, depending on the size of the cuttlefish.

Chop into bite-sized chunks and pour over the remaining parsley oil. Serve with the lemon wedges.

SEPIA CON SOBRASADA ★ O CHORIZO ★

CUTTLEFISH WITH SOBRASADA SAUSAGE OR CHORIZO

SERVES 4

1 MEDIUM TO LARGE CUTTLEFISH, CLEANED (ASK YOUR FISHMONGER TO DO THIS FOR YOU)

OLIVE OIL, FOR FRYING

1 ONION, FINELY CHOPPED

2 BAY LEAVES

130G (4½OZ) SOBRASADA DE MALLORCA OR CURED CHORIZO SAUSAGE, CHOPPED SMALL

200ML (¾ CUP) WHITE WINE

150G (HEAPED ½ CUP) TOMATO PASSATA (OR STRAINED OR MILLED CANNED TOMATOES)

NOTE
Sobrasada sausage can be found online, but if you can't get hold of any, blend some chorizo into a paste with a drizzle of olive oil in a food processor.

This stew is not very well known in mainland Spain, however it is a typical dish in the Balearic Islands, specifically in Mallorca, where the traditional Sobrasada sausage comes from. This product is very special; if I had to describe it it would be as a chorizo pâté. Cuttlefish is soft and delicate and therefore quick and easy to cook, making this delicious dish really simple to make.

Cut the cleaned cuttlefish into small pieces about 2.5cm (1in) wide.

Heat some olive oil in a medium-sized pan over a medium heat and sauté the onion with the bay leaves. If you are using chorizo sausage, this would be the time to add it. Once the onion is transparent and soft, add the cuttlefish pieces, stir once and immediately pour over the wine. Cook over a high heat for at least 1 minute, until the alcohol has evaporated, then add the passata and cook for a further 3 minutes.

Using your hands, soften the Sobrasada, if using, and add it to the stew. Keep stirring to make sure all the ingredients are well mixed and cook for a further 2 minutes, then serve.

★ VIEIRAS GRATINADAS ★

SCALLOP AND SERRANO HAM GRATIN SERVED IN THE SHELL

SERVES 4 AS A TAPA

8 SCALLOPS IN THEIR SHELLS
(YOU CAN ASK YOUR FISHMONGER
TO OPEN THEM FOR YOU)

275ML (1 CUP + 2½ TBSP) WHOLE MILK

30G (2 TBSP) BUTTER

¼ ONION, FINELY CHOPPED

30G (1OZ) SERRANO HAM,
FINELY CHOPPED

30G (3⅝ TBSP) PLAIN
(ALL-PURPOSE) FLOUR

A PINCH OF SALT

A PINCH OF WHITE PEPPER

4 TBSP BREADCRUMBS

1 SALTED ANCHOVY

1 SPRIG FRESH PARSLEY

I've noticed that scallops are more common in the UK than they are in Spain. I can see them in almost any restaurant and the variations are endless. In my country we don't eat them that much. This is perhaps because we have a larger variety of other seafood available. Having said that, this recipe carries a flavour punch. For those who hate anchovies, don't let the anchovy in the breadcrumbs put you off; trust me when I say that after cooking the anchovy will not taste anything like it does when you take it out of the tin.

Open the scallops and use a sharp knife to separate the meat from the shell. Scrap any ugly bits so that you're left with the white meat and the red roe. If you don't like the roe, just remove it. Wash the shells and scallops, pat dry with kitchen paper and set aside.

Warm the milk in a small pan over a low heat. Preheat the grill (broiler) to hot.

Melt the butter in a medium pan over a medium heat and fry the onion and ham for a few minutes until the onion is soft and transparent. Add the flour and cook for 5 more minutes, stirring continuously, until the flour has a light toasted colour. Add the warmed milk, little by little, and the salt and pepper, stirring all the time until you have a smooth and silky white sauce. Lower the heat and simmer for about 15 minutes, stirring so that the sauce doesn't stick to the pan.

Tip the breadcrumbs, anchovy and parsley into a food processor and blend.

Line up the shells on a baking sheet and place a scallop on each shell. Cover with a couple of spoonfuls of the ham béchamel and sprinkle over the anchovy breadcrumbs. Grill for 5 minutes and serve hot.

HUEVOS Y AVES

EGGS & POULTRY

★ HUEVOS A LA FLAMENCA ★

BAKED EGGS WITH HAM IN TOMATO SAUCE

SERVES 4 AS A TAPA

300G (2 CUPS FRESH OR 2½ CUPS FROZEN) PEAS

300G (10½OZ) ASPARAGUS OR 1 RED OR GREEN (BELL) PEPPER, CHOPPED

50ML (3½ TBSP) OLIVE OIL

2 GARLIC CLOVES, THINLY SLICED

1 MEDIUM ONION, FINELY CHOPPED

4 SLICES SERRANO HAM OR 1 CHORIZO SAUSAGE, CHOPPED

1 X 400-G TIN (SCANT 2 CUPS) CHOPPED (DICED) TOMATOES

A PINCH OF SUGAR

½ TSP SWEET PIMENTÓN (SWEET SMOKED PAPRIKA)

½ TSP HOT PIMENTÓN (HOT SMOKED PAPRIKA)

1 TBSP FINELY CHOPPED FRESH PARSLEY, PLUS A LITTLE EXTRA TO GARNISH

4 EGGS (OR 8 IF YOU ARE REALLY HUNGRY)

SALT AND FRESHLY GROUND BLACK PEPPER

BREAD, TO SERVE

NOTE
Duck eggs work really well in this dish; they have that extra bit of flavour and, as we know, size does matter.

This traditional Andalusian dish can be prepared in a snip and is ideal for chucking in whatever ingredients you happen to have in the fridge – plenty of veggies, a bit of ham (bacon or chorizo) and eggs. Just a few staples thrown together.

Preheat the oven to 180°C/350°F/gas mark 4.

Prepare a saucepan with boiling water and add the peas, asparagus and a pinch of salt. Boil for 2 minutes, then drain and rinse with cold water to stop the vegetables from cooking. Set aside.

Put the olive oil in a frying pan over a medium heat. Add the garlic and fry for a few seconds before adding the chopped onion and the ham or chorizo. Cook for about 5 minutes and then add the asparagus and peas. Cook for a further 5 minutes before adding the chopped tomatoes, sugar, sweet pimentón, hot pimentón and a pinch of salt (don't over season at this point as the ham or chorizo will release more salt when baking). Cook it for 10 minutes over a low heat. Add the parsley.

Pour into a medium ovenproof dish or 4 individual dishes, crack the eggs over the top and season. Bake for 7–8 minutes or until the egg is cooked to your liking. Garnish with a little finely chopped fresh parsley and serve with good bread.

★ REVUELTO DE SETAS ★

SCRAMBLED EGGS WITH WILD MUSHROOMS

SERVES 2

A DRIZZLE OF OLIVE OIL

1 SMALL PIECE CHILLI OR CAYENNE PEPPER, FINELY CHOPPED

200G (3 CUPS) WILD MUSHROOMS OR A MIXTURE OF OYSTER AND SHIITAKE, CHOPPED

2 GARLIC CLOVES, SLICED

4 EGGS

SALT AND FRESHLY GROUND BLACK PEPPER

Scrambled eggs is a star dish for a weekend breakfast for most people in the UK; in Spain we prefer to have it for dinner (I prefer churros for breakfast). We add more ingredients, such as mushrooms, spinach or even prawns, and that is what boosts a nutritional dinner and makes the eggs into something a bit more filling.

Heat the olive oil in a pan over a medium heat and fry the chopped chilli pepper for 30 seconds. Add the mushrooms and a pinch of salt and sauté for 3–4 minutes. Add the sliced garlic and fry for a couple more minutes.

Crack all the eggs on top of the mushrooms and stir together until the eggs look smooth and are still runny. I do not recommend beating the eggs first. Remove from the heat – the remaining heat will keep the eggs cooking until they're done. Season with salt and black pepper and serve.

★ TORTILLA FRANCESA ★

NOT JUST ANOTHER FRENCH OMELETTE

SERVES 1

3 ORGANIC, FREE-RANGE EGGS

1 TSP EXTRA VIRGIN OLIVE OIL

A PINCH OF SALT

What if I told you that I was taught how to make this French omelette while working for Ferran Adrià, and that I promise to you I have never tried a French omelette this good in my life – would that be enough to catch your attention with such a simple dish? Next time you need to cook an omelette, do me a favour and remember you read this, then read it again and try it.

Crack the eggs into a bowl, making sure there is no shell in it. Whisk lightly with a fork for no longer than 30 seconds.

Place a large, non-stick frying pan over a low-medium heat. Pour the olive oil over the pan and use folded kitchen paper to spread the oil all over the surface of the pan, coating every single corner of it. Be careful not to burn the tips of your fingers.

The pan shouldn't be too hot. This is one of the keys to a great omelette, which should cook slowly and in layers, like crêpes.

Sprinkle the salt into the eggs and whisk for 5 more seconds, then pour them into the pan.

After 10 seconds, and with the help of a flexible spatula, fold one side into the other to form a half-moon shape. Tilt the pan over the empty half so that it fills with runny egg again to form another layer. Fold the other half into the newly forming layer and tilt the pan over the empty side to fill it again and form another layer.

Turn off the heat so that the last 2 layers cook with the residual heat. Just repeat the process as many or as few times as needed until there is no runny egg remaining to coat the pan when you tilt it.

Fold the omelette and enjoy right away.

HUEVOS CON CHORIZO
★ BENEDICTINOS ★

EGGS BENEDICT WITH SPINACH AND CHORIZO HOLLANDAISE

SERVES 4

2 FRESH SPANISH CHORIZO SAUSAGES (PREFERABLY LIGHTLY SMOKED), FINELY CHOPPED

450G (2 CUPS) UNSALTED BUTTER

4–8 EGGS, PLUS 5 YOLKS

JUICE FROM ½ LEMON

2 TBSP EXTRA VIRGIN OLIVE OIL

1 GARLIC CLOVE, FINELY CHOPPED

250G (4½ CUPS) BABY SPINACH

SALT AND FRESHLY GROUND BLACK PEPPER

4 SLICES TOASTED BRIOCHE, TO SERVE

SWEET PIMENTÓN (SWEET SMOKED PAPRIKA), TO SERVE

Eggs Benedict are unbeatable, the perfect brunch to me. Not Spanish at all, but when I made the chorizo hollandaise for the first time I swear I thought I had just changed the world forever. I thought to myself 'I have just brought eggs Benedict to a whole other level'. I was full of pride. I don't want to sound arrogant but, honestly, my weekend mornings haven't been the same again since.

Heat a frying pan over a medium heat and dry-fry the chorizo for 3–4 minutes. Add the butter and melt.

Pour some water into a small saucepan over a medium heat. Add the egg yolks, lemon juice, 2 tablespoons water and a pinch of salt to a heatproof bowl slightly larger than the saucepan. Rest the bowl over the saucepan and whisk for about 2 minutes or until it gets fluffy, taking care not to overcook it. While whisking, slowly add the chorizo butter in a thin stream until the sauce has fully emulsified and has a creamy mayonnaise texture. Add a touch of salt and pepper and set aside.

Heat the oil in a pan over a medium heat and fry the garlic for a few seconds before adding the baby spinach. Cook for 1 minute to allow the spinach leaves to wilt. Season with salt and pepper and set aside.

Lay the toasted brioche slices on serving plates and top each with a spoonful of spinach.

One at a time, break each egg into a ramekin and pour into a pan of simmering water. Gently poach for 2–3 minutes, remove with a slotted spoon and place 1 or 2 eggs on top of each brioche. To finish, spoon the warm chorizo hollandaise over the poached eggs and sprinkle pimentón over each one.

ALITAS DE POLLO
★ A LA MIEL Y LIMON ★
LEMON AND HONEY CHICKEN WINGS

SERVES 4

400G (14OZ) CHICKEN WINGS

1 LEMON

3 TBSP EXTRA VIRGIN OLIVE OIL

4 SPRIGS FRESH THYME

1 HEAD OF GARLIC, CUT IN HALF

A PINCH OF SWEET PIMENTÓN
(SWEET SMOKED PAPRIKA)

3 TBSP HONEY

2 TBSP CHOPPED FRESH
CORIANDER (CILANTRO) LEAVES

SEA SALT AND FRESHLY
GROUND BLACK PEPPER

I am yet to meet someone who doesn't like chicken wings. Traditionally this recipe was made using the whole chicken, however it is so much more shareable when made with wings.

Bring a pan of water to the boil, add the chicken wings and boil for 5 minutes. Remove and drain on kitchen paper for 5 minutes.

Meanwhile, zest the lemon, halve it and squeeze out the juice, but don't throw the rest of it away.

Heat the oil in a frying pan over a high heat. Add the thyme sprigs, chicken wings, squeezed lemon halves and the garlic and fry for a couple of minutes on each side. Sprinkle the pimentón over the chicken and after 10 seconds drizzle the lemon juice and honey into the pan. Season with salt and pepper.

Continue to sauté the chicken until cooked through, allowing the liquid to reduce while making sure the wings are fully coated in the glaze. Add the lemon zest right at the end as it turns bitter if added too early and loses its fragrance quite quickly.

Sprinkle with the chopped coriander and sea salt before serving.

★ POLLASTRE AL AST ★

SPANISH-STYLE ROAST CHICKEN

SERVES 2

1 SMALL FREE-RANGE CHICKEN

2 TBSP LARD OR OLIVE OIL

1 TSP SALT

2 GENEROUS PINCHES OF
BLACK PEPPER

2 TBSP HERBES DE PROVENCE

This is proper street food for us in Spain. You will find the biggest rotisseries I've ever seen in street food markets across the country on the weekends, packed with beautifully golden and crispy little chickens, intoxicating the markets with their beautiful aroma. It is always the last stop before you go home after your grocery shopping. Simplicity at its best and so easy to make at home.

Preheat the oven to 200°C/400°F/gas mark 6.

Clean the whole chicken inside and out with water and dry properly, then rub the entire chicken, inside and out, with the lard. Season with the salt, black pepper and herbs, again inside and outside.

Fill an tall, empty can such as a beer can with water and stand it in the middle of a roasting tray. Stand the chicken on the can, inserting it into the cavity, so that the wings point up and the drumsticks hang down. This will allow air to circulate around the chicken.

Place the tray on the lowest rack of the oven and cook for 20 minutes, then reduce the heat to 160°C/325°F/gas mark 3 and cook for a further 45 minutes, or until ready. The skin should be very crispy but the meat should still be very moist inside, with the juices running clear.

See photograph on page 88.

★ PINCHOS DE POLLO ★

MARINATED CHICKEN SKEWERS

SERVES 4

600G (1LB 5OZ) BONELESS AND
SKINLESS CHICKEN THIGHS

3 SPRIGS FRESH CORIANDER
(CILANTRO), FINELY CHOPPED

1 GARLIC CLOVE, FINELY CHOPPED

4 TBSP OLIVE OIL

1 TBSP HONEY

GRATED ZEST AND JUICE OF 1 LEMON

1 TBSP SWEET PIMENTÓN
(SWEET SMOKED PAPRIKA)

1 TSP GROUND TURMERIC

1 TSP GROUND CUMIN

A PINCH OF GROUND BLACK PEPPER

12 X 18-CM (7-IN) WOODEN SKEWERS,
SOAKED IN WATER FOR 10 MINUTES

The best thing about these skewers is that they can be prepared well in advance if you are making a BBQ, so there will be no hassle when you fire up the grill.

Cut each chicken thigh into 6 even-sized pieces and place in a non-metallic bowl.

Mix together all the rest of the ingredients to make a marinade and pour over the chicken. Mix it all together, cover with plastic wrap and leave to marinate in the fridge for at least 30 minutes or up to 3 days.

Preheat the oven to 200°C/400°F/gas mark 6.

Thread 6 pieces of chicken onto each skewer and season generously with salt.

Roast for about 10 minutes, or until cooked through.

NOTE
You can of course replace the chicken thighs in this recipe with pork, lamb, turkey or whichever meat you prefer.

★ CODORNICES CON ROMESCO ★

SPATCHCOCKED QUAIL WITH A ROASTED NUT SAUCE

SERVES 4

4 QUAIL

1 LEMON, QUARTERED, TO SERVE

FOR THE ROMESCO SAUCE

3 PIMIENTOS CHORICEROS (SPANISH
DRIED PEPPERS), CHOPPED, OPTIONAL

1 RED (BELL) PEPPER

3 TOMATOES

½ HEAD OF GARLIC, PEELED
AND CLOVES SEPARATED

100ML (⅓ CUP) OLIVE OIL

50G (HEAPED ⅓ CUP) BLANCHED
ALMONDS (OR SKIN ON)

30G (¼ CUP) BLANCHED HAZELNUTS
(OR PINE NUTS OR MORE ALMONDS)

1 SLICE BREAD

3 TBSP SHERRY VINEGAR

A PINCH OF SWEET PIMENTÓN
(SWEET SMOKED PAPRIKA)

A PINCH OF ROCK OR SEA SALT

FOR THE MARINADE

10 SPRIGS FRESH THYME,
LEAVES FINELY CHOPPED

4 GARLIC CLOVES, FINELY CHOPPED

1 TBSP SALT

2 TSP SWEET OR SPICY PIMENTÓN
(SWEET OR HOT SMOKED PAPRIKA)

2 TSP DRIED OREGANO

2 TSP GROUND CUMIN

75ML (5 TBSP) OLIVE OIL

NOTE
Romesco can also
be enjoyed with
grilled or boiled
veg or pan-fried fish.

It is generally when the sun is out that spatch-cocking comes in handy to get perfectly cooked birds, and this dish is ideal cooked over a barbecue, although it's just as good under the grill (broiler). This recipe and the accompanying sauce will be a great addition to your summer grilling repertoire.

Soak the pimientos choriceros for the romesco sauce in water for 2 hours.

Preheat the oven to 200°C/400°F/gas mark 6.

Tip the vegetables for the romesco sauce onto a roasting tray and rub with the olive oil. Roast for 25 minutes, adding the nuts and the slice of bread for the last 10 minutes of cooking. Set aside to cool slightly and then peel the vegetables and blend with the bread, nuts, sherry vinegar, pimentón, salt and pimientos choriceros, if using (by pestle, hand blender or food processor) until you have a smooth paste.

Lay a quail on a chopping board and use a sharp knife to cut the rib cage wide open. Discard the chest bone, flip over the quail and flatten it against the board. Insert 2 skewers diagonally in a cross formation from the wing to the leg, passing through the breast so that you have a completely flat bird. Repeat with the rest of the quail.

Mix together the ingredients for the marinade and brush all over the quail.

Preheat the grill (broiler) or barbecue to hot or place a griddle pan over a high heat and cook the quail to your liking, no longer than 5 minutes on each side and ideally so that it is still pinkish and juicy in the middle.

Serve each of the quail with a lemon wedge and a spoonful of romesco sauce.

★ PATO CON CIRUELAS ★

DUCK WITH PRUNES, CHESTNUTS AND PEDRO XIMENEZ SHERRY

SERVES 6

3 TBSP OLIVE OIL

1 SMALL WHOLE DUCK (ABOUT 1.5KG [3¼LB]), CLEANED

8 GARLIC CLOVES, SKIN ON BUT CRUSHED

A HANDFUL OF PEELED CHESTNUTS

1 ONION, THINLY SLICED

6 SPRIGS FRESH THYME

12 PRUNES

125ML (½ CUP) SWEET PEDRO XIMÉNEZ SHERRY

SALT AND FRESHLY GROUND BLACK PEPPER

BREAD OR ROASTED NEW POTATOES, TO SERVE

NOTE
For a really delicious accompaniment, cook the duck sitting over 600g (1lb 5oz) new potatoes so that the potatoes roast in the sauce and meat juices.

This dish has all the elements of the perfect Christmas centrepiece, if it wasn't for the fact that it is just too easy to prepare. You know how complicated we like to make it when it comes to Christmas – nothing can take half an hour.

Preheat the oven to 200°C/400°F/gas mark 6.

Heat the olive oil in a wide ovenproof pan or casserole dish over a medium heat. Season the duck with salt and pepper and pan-fry on all sides until golden. Help yourself with a pair of tongs. After 10 minutes, remove the duck from the pan and set aside.

Add the garlic cloves, chestnuts and onion to the pan and fry for 10 minutes. Add the thyme and prunes and cook for a further 5 minutes. Return the duck to the pan and flambé with the sherry. To do this, slowly tilt the pan towards the flame until the sherry catches, or light with a match. Let the flames flare up then die down and then add 250ml (1 cup) water.

Put the pan in the oven and cook for 25 minutes, then switch off the heat and leave the duck in the oven for a further 20 minutes without opening the door. This should crisp up the skin and cook the duck to perfection as well as resting the meat.

Serve as a centrepiece with some good bread or roasted new potatoes.

VERDURAS

{ VEGETABLES }

★ ESPARRAGOS CON JAMON ★

GREEN ASPARAGUS WITH SERRANO HAM

SERVES 3 AS A TAPA

1 BUNCH GREEN ASPARAGUS

A DRIZZLE OF OLIVE OIL

2 GARLIC CLOVES, THINLY SLICED

2 SLICES SERRANO HAM, CHOPPED, PLUS 1 SLICE TO SERVE

A PINCH OF SEA SALT

A PINCH OF FRESHLY GROUND BLACK PEPPER

25ML (1 TBSP + 2 TSP) DRY SHERRY WINE OR A SPLASH OF SHERRY VINEGAR

50G (2OZ) MANCHEGO CHEESE, SLICED

When asparagus is in season, it's a big event every year. Everyone promotes it with pride, whether on the supermarket shelves or high up on restaurant menus. It is a very special veggie to me. I love its flavour and versatility, since it just goes well with so many other foods. In Spain it's very common to find it served with ham – simple and delicious.

Snap off the hard ends of the asparagus and blanch the spears for 2 minutes in a pan of boiling hot water. Depending on the thickness of the asparagus you may need a bit longer to get them cooked.

Heat the oil in a frying pan over a medium heat and cook the garlic and the chopped ham until the garlic is golden. Add the blanched asparagus, season with the salt and pepper and sauté for 30 seconds, then flambé with the dry sherry wine. To do this, slowly tilt the pan towards the flame until the wine catches, or light with a match. Let the flames flare up then die down. Serve with the sliced Manchego and a slice of ham.

VARIATION

If you ever come across fresh Spanish white asparagus in a market, please buy them. They are very temperamental and need to be very fresh or they get tough and bitter. But young and fresh they are a real treat. You can make this dish with white asparagus by boiling them for at least 10 minutes longer than green ones with a tablespoon of sugar and a knob of butter in the water.

★ PISTO RIOJANO ★

MIXED FRIED VEGETABLES

SERVES 4

2 MEDIUM, RIPE TOMATOES
(300G [10½OZ] IN TOTAL)

2 MEDIUM GREEN ROMANO
OR (BELL) PEPPERS

1 RED ONION

1 MEDIUM COURGETTE (ZUCCHINI)

1 POTATO

50ML (3½ TBSP) EXTRA VIRGIN
OLIVE OIL

1 TSP SALT

1 GARLIC CLOVE, SLICED

1 TSP SUGAR

2 EGGS

Across Spain there are several ways of cooking *pisto*, a warming and very tasty traditional vegetable stew that's similar to the French ratatouille. This one is typical of La Rioja in north-eastern Spain, where our famous red wine comes from. The peculiarity of this stew is the cooked eggs, as they are eaten like scrambled eggs. You could also poach them.

Peel and seed the tomatoes and chop the flesh into 1-cm (⅜-in) cubes along with the peppers, onion, courgette and potato.

Heat the olive oil in a large saucepan over a medium heat and add the salt, then the cubed onions, garlic and peppers. Cover, reduce the heat to low and sweat for at least 15 minutes, stirring occasionally.

Meanwhile, parboil the diced potatoes for about 7 minutes in boiling water and set aside.

Once the onion and peppers are soft, add the chopped tomatoes, sugar, courgette and parboiled potatoes to the pan, increase the heat to medium and fry for another 10 minutes.

Beat the eggs and add them to the hot stew, stirring until they scramble and set with the vegetables – delicious!

PIQUILLOS
★ RELLENOS DE SETAS ★
PIQUILLO PEPPERS STUFFED WITH MUSHROOMS

SERVES 6 AS A TAPA

150G (5OZ) WILD MUSHROOMS, SUCH AS OYSTER, OR A MIXTURE OF FIELD MUSHROOMS

50ML (3½ TBSP) OLIVE OIL

¼ SMALL ONION, FINELY CHOPPED

2 GARLIC CLOVES, FINELY CHOPPED

2 SPRIGS FRESH THYME

A SPLASH OF WHITE WINE

30G (2 TBSP) BUTTER

30G (3⅔ TBSP) PLAIN (ALL-PURPOSE) FLOUR

400ML (1¾ CUPS) WHOLE MILK, HOT

A PINCH OF GRATED NUTMEG

15 TINNED PIQUILLO PEPPERS

400ML (1¾ CUPS) DOUBLE (HEAVY) CREAM

50G (½ CUP) GRATED CHEDDAR CHEESE, PLUS EXTRA FOR TOPPING

SALT AND FRESHLY GROUND BLACK PEPPER

BREAD, TO SERVE

I have always been a big fan of mushrooms in all their forms – from taking long walks with family to pick wild mushrooms, to cooking them in many ways at home. This recipe is packed full of tastiness.

Trim the mushrooms, removing the stalks, and wipe them with a damp cloth. Roughly chop. Heat the olive oil in a large frying pan over a high heat and fry the mushrooms for at least 2 minutes, season with salt and pepper, stir well and season again. Fry for a further 2 minutes. Add the onion and cook for 1 minute. Add the garlic, thyme and cook for 2 minutes, then add the wine and cook for 1 minute.

Lower the heat to medium and add the butter. Let it melt, then add the flour and cook for 5 minutes, stirring constantly, until the flour is lightly toasted. Add the hot milk, little by little, and the nutmeg, whisking until you have a smooth and silky white sauce. Simmer for about 20 minutes, stirring from time to time to make sure it doesn't catch on the bottom of the pan, until the sauce has thickened. Pour into a bowl and cover with plastic wrap. Chill completely in the fridge. After at least 2 hours, the béchamel should be firm and ready to handle.

Preheat the oven to 160°C/325°F/gas mark 3.

Bring 3 of the piquillo peppers, the cream and cheese to the boil in a small pan over a medium heat and cook for 10 minutes. Season with salt and pepper. Use a hand blender to blend until smooth.

Using a spoon, fill the remaining 12 piquillo peppers with the mushroom béchamel. Lay them in an oven dish and pour the piquillo sauce on top. Scatter some more grated chese over the top. Bake for 15 minutes until lightly browned and crispy on top. Serve with bread.

See photographs on following pages.

★ BERENJENAS FRITAS CON MIEL ★

AUBERGINES WITH HONEY

SERVES 4 AS A TAPA

1 AUBERGINE (EGGPLANT)

285ML (1¼ CUPS) WHOLE MILK

2 TBSP DARK MUSCOVADO SUGAR

2 TBSP HONEY

1 EGG YOLK

15ML (1 TBSP) LAGER

2 TBSP PLAIN (ALL-PURPOSE) FLOUR

1 TSP SEA SALT

400ML (1¾ CUPS) SUNFLOWER OIL,
FOR DEEP-FRYING

I am sure you'll love this one. In Córdoba and Malaga, southern Spain, this is a classic and whenever I've put it on one of my restaurant menus, everyone has loved it.

Cut the aubergine into batons as if they were fat-cut chips (or round slices, half moons... it makes no difference) and place in a bowl. Pour over the milk, completely submerging the aubergine, and set aside for at least 30 minutes. This will remove any sourness from the aubergine.

Melt the muscovado and honey together in a small pan over a low heat for 5 minutes. It doesn't need cooking, just melting.

Meanwhile, beat the egg yolk in a clean mixing bowl until it is soft and airy. Add the beer (I just gave you a reason to drink the rest) and flour, stirring with a whisk to make sure it is all properly mixed. Leave to rest for 15 minutes and then add the salt and stir until it is well combined with the mixture.

Heat the oil in a tall-sided pan over a medium-high heat until a cube of day-old bread dropped into the oil turns golden in about 30 seconds. Alternatively, heat a deep fryer to 180°C (360°F). The oil should not be too hot or smoking.

Drain the aubergine and coat it with the batter mixture. Deep-fry in batches, perhaps 3 or 4 batons at a time, until they have a nice golden colour, and then drain on kitchen paper.

Serve the aubergine batons with a good drizzle of the muscovado honey over the top.

CALABACIN
★ A LA MALLORQUINA ★
STUFFED COURGETTES

SERVES 6

6 LARGE COURGETTES (ZUCCHINI)

OLIVE OIL, FOR FRYING

1 LARGE ONION, FINELY CHOPPED

4 GARLIC CLOVES, CRUSHED

250G (9OZ) MINCED (GROUND) PORK

250G (9OZ) MINCED (GROUND) BEEF

2 TBSP TOMATO PURÉE (PASTE)

3 SPRIGS FRESH THYME

2–3 FRESH MARJORAM LEAVES
(OR 1 TSP DRIED OREGANO)

330ML (1¼ CUPS + 2 TBSP) LAGER

2 TSP CORNFLOUR (CORNSTARCH)

1 EGG YOLK

125ML (½ CUP) MILK

100G (2 CUPS) BREADCRUMBS

SALT AND FRESHLY GROUND
BLACK PEPPER

This is my version of the better-known aubergines Mallorca-style. I've chosen courgettes here instead because I think their meat is more delicate and natural and this complements the heavy meat filling better.

Cut the courgettes in half lengthways and use a spoon to scoop out the flesh. Finely chop the flesh and set it and the halved courgettes aside.

Heat a drizzle of oil in a pan over a medium heat and add the onion, garlic and chopped courgette. Cook until soft and golden, making sure the vegetables don't burn. Add all the meat, the tomato purée, salt and pepper, thyme and marjoram and cook for about 10 minutes, stirring vigorously for the first 2 minutes so that the meat breaks up into small pieces. When the meat is cooked through, pour over the beer and let simmer for about 30 minutes for the liquid to completely reduce down.

In a bowl, add the cornflour and egg yolk to the cold milk and beat until the cornflour dilutes. Add this mixture to the meat and stir for 1–2 minutes until the sauce thickens up and then remove from the heat right away.

Preheat the oven to 180°C/350°F/gas mark 4.

Fill the courgette skins with the meat mixture, sprinkle breadcrumbs over the top and bake for 20 minutes, until the breadcrumbs are crisp and golden and the courgette boats have cooked through.

COLIFLOR CON AJOS
★ VINAGRE Y ALCAPARRAS ★
CAULIFLOWER WITH GARLIC, VINEGAR AND CAPERS

SERVES 4 AS A TAPA

1 LARGE CAULIFLOWER, BROKEN INTO FLORETS AND LEAVES RESERVED

200ML (¾ CUP) MILK

EXTRA VIRGIN OLIVE OIL, FOR FRYING

5 GARLIC CLOVES, GERM DISCARDED (SEE NOTE BELOW) AND SLICED

50G (5 TBSP) DRAINED CAPERS

1 TSP CUMIN SEEDS

½ TSP SWEET PIMENTÓN (SWEET SMOKED PAPRIKA)

50ML (3½ TBSP) SHERRY OR OTHER WHITE VINEGAR

SALT

NOTE

I always like to remove the germ from inside the garlic clove to make the flavour less aggressive. In young cloves it is soft and tender but as it grows older it turns bitter. Slice the clove in half and pry out the central germ with a small knife or your fingernail.

This takes just 15 minutes to make and I cook it very often at home because it's simple, light and healthy and it's full of flavour. This is a Spanish version of a Chinese stir-fry.

Place the cauliflower florets in a large pan, cover them with water and then add a pinch of salt and the milk (this will make the cauliflower whiter and prevent odours). Cook over a high heat until al dente, about 8 minutes in total (from the time you put the cauliflower in the pan), drain and refresh under cold running water. Set aside.

Pour a good drizzle of oil into a cold frying pan, add the reserved cauliflower leaves, sliced garlic, capers and cumin seeds and then turn the heat to high. When the garlic turns golden, add the pimentón and then the sherry vinegar. Reduce the liquid for 30 seconds and then toss the cauliflower into the pan. Make sure the ingredients are well mixed and serve.

★ HABAS CON CHORIZO ★

BROAD BEANS WITH CHORIZO

SERVES 4 AS A TAPA

250G (2 CUPS) SHELLED BROAD
(FAVA) BEANS (IF YOU FIND BABY
BROAD BEANS, EVEN BETTER)

50ML (3½ TBSP) EXTRA VIRGIN
OLIVE OIL

¼ ONION, FINELY CHOPPED

5 GARLIC CLOVES, SKIN ON
BUT CRUSHED

1 SPRIG FRESH OREGANO

1 CHORIZO COOKING
(FRESH UNCOOKED) SAUSAGE
(ABOUT 90G [3½OZ]), CHOPPED

GRATED ZEST AND JUICE OF ½ LEMON

SEA SALT AND FRESHLY GROUND
BLACK PEPPER

BREAD, TO SERVE

Broad (fava) beans are widely consumed all over
Spain. We love to eat them in many ways: in stews,
soups, and paellas, or even raw and salted as a snack.
The tender seeds within the pod are delicious.
The younger they are, the better, but obviously
the more expensive, too.

Bring a large pan of salted water to the boil. Add
the beans, bring back to the boil and then cook for
2 minutes. Drain and rinse with cold running water.
Set aside.

Heat the olive oil in a frying pan over a medium
heat and add the onion, garlic, oregano and chorizo.
Sweat for 5 minutes until the onion is transparent
and soft. Increase the heat to high, add the broad
beans and sauté for a couple of minutes.

Add 25ml (2 Tbsp) water, the lemon zest and juice
and some seasoning, and serve with some good bread.

★ PATATAS MACHACONAS ★

SPICED MASHED POTATOES WITH CRISPY PORK BELLY

3 LARGE WAXY POTATOES
(ABOUT 500G [1LB 2 OZ]),
PEELED AND QUARTERED

1 WHOLE HEAD OF GARLIC

½ ONION

1 BAY LEAF

EXTRA VIRGIN OLIVE OIL,
FOR FRYING

300G (10½OZ) PORK BELLY,
CUT INTO BITE-SIZED CHUNKS

1 TBSP SWEET PIMENTÓN
(SWEET SMOKED PAPRIKA)

1 TSP SPICY PIMENTÓN
(HOT SMOKED PAPRIKA)

SALT AND FRESHLY GROUND
BLACK PEPPER

This traditional tapa comes from Avila in the province of Castilla, the epicentre of Spain. Castilla is a land of history, kingdoms, castles, cathedrals and an outstanding gastronomy. You could say this is a rustic mashed potato dish, spiced up with smoked pimentón and traditionally served with pork crackling.

Put the potatoes, garlic, onion, a pinch of salt and the bay leaf in a pan and cover with water. Bring to the boil and cook over a medium heat for about 25 minutes, until the potatoes are soft. Drain the potatoes, but keep a bit of the water, the garlic, onion and bay leaf. Peel the garlic and keep the pulp.

Heat a drizzle of oil in a frying pan and fry the pork belly pieces with the bay leaf from the potatoes and a bit of salt until crispy (this can take up to 30 minutes). Set the meat aside to rest.

In the same pan, fry the half-boiled onion, then set aside for later.

Fry the garlic until light golden. Add the sweet and hot pimentón and after 10 seconds add the potatoes, give them a stir and mash them in the pan with a fork. If they get too dry use the reserved cooking water to thin the purée. Season with salt and pepper.

Serve the potatoes with the crispy pork belly and pan-fried onion on top.

★ ACELGAS CON PATATAS ★

SWISS CHARD WITH POTATOES

SERVES 4

2 BUNCHES SWISS CHARD
(ABOUT 10 LEAVES), WASHED

4 WAXY POTATOES, PEELED
AND QUARTERED

FOR THE SOFRITO DE AJO DRESSING

4 TBSP EXTRA VIRGIN OLIVE OIL

4 GARLIC CLOVES, SLICED

1 TSP SWEET PIMENTÓN
(SWEET SMOKED PAPRIKA)

3 TBSP SHERRY VINEGAR

This is a healthy dish for a nutritious supper. In Spain we often use chard as it is less sweet than spinach and works well with the potatoes. You can use any kind of chard – if you can find them with red, white or yellow stems you can mix them and create a more colourful plate.

Trim the stems from the chard leaves and slice thinly. Cut the leaves into strips.

Bring a large pan of salted water to the boil over a high heat and cook the potatoes for 12 minutes, until soft but still undercooked. Add the chard stems and cook for a further 5 minutes before adding the leaves. Cook for another 3 minutes.

Drain the vegetables in a colander. Don't worry if the potatoes break or mash – if they are good waxy potatoes this will add a fantastic texture to the greens.

For the sofrito de ajo dressing, heat the extra virgin olive oil in a large frying pan over a medium heat and cook the garlic until golden. Take the pan off the heat and add the pimentón, give it a good stir and add the sherry vinegar before pouring this *sofrito* over the potatoes and chard. Mix well and serve.

BERENJENAS RELLENAS
★ DE PISTO ★

AUBERGINES FILLED WITH PISTO AND MANCHEGO

SERVES 4

2 LARGE AUBERGINES (EGGPLANTS)

100ML (⅓ CUP) OLIVE OIL, PLUS 4 TBSP

1 ONION, DICED

1 RED (BELL) PEPPER, CUT INTO CUBES

4 GARLIC CLOVES, THINLY SLICED

1 COURGETTE (ZUCCHINI),
CUT INTO CUBES

2 TOMATOES, CUT INTO CUBES

1 TSP SUGAR

A PINCH OF SWEET PIMENTÓN
(SWEET SMOKED PAPRIKA)

A PINCH OF GROUND CUMIN

50G (2OZ) MANCHEGO CHEESE,
CHOPPED

SALT

FOR THE SAUCE

1 X PUNNET BLACKBERRIES
(ABOUT 150G [HEAPED 1 CUP])

4 TBSP SUGAR

A really rich and filling vegetarian dish that can be prepared in advance for convenience. It is unusual for me to cook vegetarian meals but I did it once for a few friends, as one of them is vegetarian, and he described it as vegetarian's heaven. So there you go!

Preheat the oven to 180°C/350°F/gas mark 4 and line a baking sheet with baking parchment.

Trim straight across the top and bottom of each aubergine and then cut them in half lengthways. Stand them up and use a paring knife and teaspoon to carefully hollow out each half to make bowls, cutting close to the skin without piercing it. Cut the flesh into cubes.

Heat the oil in a large frying pan over a high heat and sauté the onion for 1 minute and then the red (bell) pepper for 2 minutes. Add the sliced garlic and after 1 minute add the aubergine and courgette cubes.

Once the vegetables have started to caramelize, add the tomato cubes, sugar, sweet pimentón, cumin and a pinch of salt and continue to sauté for 2 minutes. You should now have what we call a *pisto*. The vegetables should be cooked through, but still have some bite.

Season the aubergine bowls with salt and fill them with the *pisto*. Bake for 20 minutes, then top with the cheese and return to the oven for another 10 minutes.

Meanwhile, make the sauce. Wash and dry the blackberries and put them in a small pan over a low heat with the sugar. Heat, stirring occasionally, until the sugar has become a rich purple syrup.

Stand the aubergine bowls on a plate and spoon the blackberries and syrup over the top.

ENSALADAS

SALADS

ENSALADA DE CANONIGOS, ★ PIMIENTOS Y ATUN ★

LAMB'S LETTUCE, ROASTED RED PEPPER, OLIVE AND TUNA SALAD

SERVES 6

2 RED (BELL) PEPPERS OR 1 X 250-G
[9-OZ] JAR ROASTED RED PEPPERS

4 EGGS

4 HANDFULS LAMB'S LETTUCE
(CORN SALAD)

1 X 200-G (7-OZ) TIN/JAR GREEN
MANZANILLA OLIVES, OR OTHER
SPANISH VARIETY, DRAINED

2 TBSP SHERRY VINEGAR

1 X 170-G TIN (6-OZ CAN) TUNA IN
OLIVE OIL, SPANISH IF POSSIBLE
(WORTH EVERY EXTRA PENNY),
SHREDDED, RESERVING THE OIL

A PINCH OF SEA SALT

We love tinned foods in Spain, not just because of the flavour but because they are so convenient when you have no time; you will find all sorts of things in tins or jars in the supermarkets. This recipe could be called 'open the tin salad' – so easy, filling and great tasting.

Preheat the oven to 180°C/350°F/gas mark 4 and roast the peppers for 20 minutes, if using fresh peppers. Remove from the oven, cover with a cloth or lid and leave for 30 minutes. Peel the softened peppers over a salad bowl to capture all the juices and discard the skins. Alternatively, use ready roasted peppers.

Put the eggs in a pan of cold water and bring to the boil, cooking for about 5 minutes in total. Cool them down by running them under cold water and then peel and cut into halves. They should be firm but not overcooked – there is a fine line we should never cross.

Mix together all the ingredients in the salad bowl, season with the salt and use the olive oil from the tuna as a dressing.

See photograph on page 124.

★ ENSALADA CAMPERA ★

NEW POTATO, TUNA AND EGG SALAD

SERVES 4

4 EGGS

400G (14OZ, ABOUT 3 CUPS)
NEW POTATOES

1 TSP + A PINCH SALT

2 TOMATOES (WEIGHING 250G [9OZ]
IN TOTAL), CUT INTO WEDGES

1 RED (BELL) PEPPER, CHOPPED
INTO 1-CM [¾-IN] DICE

1 GREEN (BELL) PEPPER, CHOPPED
INTO 1-CM [¾-IN] DICE

½ RED ONION, THINLY SLICED

100G (1 CUP) GREEN AND
BLACK PITTED OLIVES

1 X 170-G TIN (6-OZ CAN) TUNA IN
OLIVE OIL

3 TBSP SHERRY VINEGAR

5 TBSP EXTRA VIRGIN OLIVE OIL

1 TBSP FINELY CHOPPED
FLAT-LEAF PARSLEY

This is one of those salads that are incredibly popular in Spanish households, not just in mine. The name translates literally as 'country' salad, so maybe it's this outdoors-y name that makes us cook it for picnics and BBQs.

Place the eggs and potatoes in a pan, add a pinch of salt and cover with cold water. Bring to the boil over a high heat and after a total of 5 minutes, take out the eggs. Cool them down by running them under cold water and then peel and cut into quarters. The potatoes shouldn't take longer than 20 minutes to cook, but check them after 15 minutes by piercing them with a paring knife. If they feel soft inside, drain and set aside to cool down, then cut in half and place in a big salad bowl.

Add the tomato wedges, diced peppers, sliced red onion and olives to the bowl and mix together with all the ingredients. Open the tin of tuna and use the fishy olive oil from the tin to dress the salad, as well as adding a generous amount of salt, the sherry vinegar and extra virgin olive oil, and give it all a really good stir.

Sprinkle the finely chopped parsley and egg quarters over the top and serve.

ENSALADA DE AGUACATE ★ Y CALABAZA ASADA ★

SALAD OF AVOCADO, LETTUCE, BUTTERNUT SQUASH AND WALNUTS

SERVES 6

1 SMALL BUTTERNUT SQUASH (TOTAL WEIGHT ABOUT 500G [1LB 2OZ]), CUT INTO SLIM WEDGES

A GOOD DRIZZLE OF EXTRA VIRGIN OLIVE OIL

2 HEADS LITTLE GEM LETTUCE, LEAVES SEPARATED

2 AVOCADOS, PEELED, STONED AND CUT INTO CHUNKS

100G (HEAPED 1 CUP) WALNUT HALVES

A FEW FRESH CORIANDER (CILANTRO) LEAVES, TO GARNISH

SALT

FOR THE VINAIGRETTE

GRATED ZEST AND JUICE OF 1 LEMON

1 TBSP WHISKY

1 TBSP HONEY

1 TSP SALT

50ML (3½ TBSP) EXTRA VIRGIN OLIVE OIL

Salads don't have to be garnishes, sides or starters. Once a week I always have a big plate of salad as a main course and nothing else. This one will fill you up, big time.

Preheat the oven to 150°C/300°F/gas mark 2 and line a baking sheet with baking parchment.

Rub the butternut squash in the olive oil and some salt, spread out on the baking sheet and bake for 30 minutes. Allow to cool.

Combine the lemon zest and juice, whisky, honey and salt for the vinaigrette in a small bowl and whisk for 1 minute. Slowly pour in the olive oil in a thin, steady stream, whisking until the vinaigrette has emulsified.

Place the cooled butternut squash, the lettuce, avocados and two-thirds of the walnut halves into a salad bowl and mix to combine. Roughly chop the rest of the walnuts and sprinkle over the salad. Drizzle with the vinaigrette and garnish with the coriander leaves.

ENSALADA DE COGOLLOS, ★ CALAMAR Y PIQUILLOS ★

HOT PAN-FRIED SQUID, LETTUCE AND PIQUILLO PEPPER SALAD

SERVES 4 AS A TAPA

300G (10½OZ) FRESH SQUID, CLEANED (YOU CAN ASK YOUR FISHMONGER TO DO THIS FOR YOU)

2 GARLIC CLOVES, VERY FINELY CHOPPED

A FEW LEAVES OF FLAT-LEAF PARSLEY, VERY FINELY CHOPPED

2 TBSP OLIVE OIL, PLUS EXTRA FOR FRYING

JUICE OF 1 LEMON

1 HEAD LITTLE GEM LETTUCE, LEAVES SEPARATED

½ X 220-G (7-OZ) TIN/JAR PIQUILLO PEPPERS

50G (⅓ CUP) PITTED BLACK OLIVES

SALT AND FRESHLY GROUND BLACK PEPPER

At home in winter time you don't feel like eating as many salads as you do in the summer. This recipe will feel very healthy in the winter months and at the same time it will warm you and fill you up like a main course.

Open the squid tube and score the inside in a cross-hatch pattern, then cut into small rectangular pieces.

Mix together the very finely chopped garlic and flat-leaf parsley, 2 tablespoons of the olive oil, the lemon juice and some salt and pepper to make a vinaigrette.

Place a large frying pan over a high heat and drizzle with more olive oil. Season the squid and pan-fry for a couple of minutes. Set aside. Add a bit more oil to the pan and cook the lettuce leaves for a few seconds.

Place the piquillo peppers, olives, squid and lettuce leaves on a plate. Drizzle the vinaigrette over the top and enjoy while still warm.

★ ENSALADILLA RUSA ★

RUSSIAN POTATO SALAD

SERVES 6 AS A TAPA

4 POTATOES (ABOUT 500G [1LB 2OZ] IN TOTAL), SKIN ON

2 EGGS

4 MEDIUM CARROTS, PEELED

A HANDFUL GARDEN PEAS

1 X 160-G TIN (6-OZ CAN) TUNA IN BRINE, DRAINED AND SHREDDED

4 SMALL PICKLED CORNICHONS, FINELY CHOPPED

ABOUT 20 PITTED GREEN OLIVES, HALVED

200G (¾ CUP) MAYONNAISE (SEE PAGE 26)

SALT

This summery dish is the Russian version of the classic potato salad. Although the original recipe contained pheasant and caviar, the Spaniards managed to create a more cost-effective recipe, replacing the meat and other expensive ingredients with tinned tuna, peas or carrots. There are several variations on this salad, which can be prepared ahead and kept in the fridge for two or three days. It is delicious as a starter or as a tapa with toast.

Put the whole potatoes, eggs and peeled carrots in a pan and cover with plenty of cold salted water. Bring to the boil over a high heat and cook for about 45 minutes, until the potatoes are soft and fully cooked. Remove the eggs from the pan after 8 minutes and the carrots after 15 minutes and run them under cold water to stop them from cooking.

Fill a small saucepan over a high heat with water and bring to the boil. Cook the peas for 2 minutes, drain and run under cold water. Cut the potatoes and carrots into 1–2-cm (⅜–¾-in) cubes. Peel and grate the eggs, or chop them with a knife.

Put the potatoes, carrots, eggs, shredded tuna, cornichons and peas into a mixing bowl with the olives. Add the Mayonnaise and mix all the ingredients until well combined.

COGOLLOS DE TUDELA
★ CON VINAGRETA DE PANCETA ★

GRILLED LETTUCE WITH A SWEET AND SOUR BACON VINAIGRETTE

SERVES 4 AS A STARTER

½ RED ONION, SLICED

4 TBSP SHERRY VINEGAR

50G (2OZ) SMOKED PANCETTA
OR BACON, DICED

A PINCH OF SWEET PIMENTÓN
(SWEET SMOKED PAPRIKA)

1 TBSP HONEY

2 HEADS LITTLE GEM LETTUCE,
SLICED IN HALF LENGTHWAYS

4 TBSP EXTRA VIRGIN OLIVE OIL

A PINCH OF SEA SALT

This is another of my mum's dishes. She has always been famous in our family for her salads – which she brings to all family gatherings. I love the concept of hot salads, particularly in winter time when you need something to warm you up.

Place the red onion in a small bowl and pour the sherry vinegar over the top. Set aside to marinate.

In a small pan over a high heat, dry-fry the pancetta or bacon until crisp. Sprinkle over the sweet pimentón and then the honey. After 30 seconds, pour over the sherry vinegar and onions to deglaze the pan. Turn the heat off under the pan and leave to sit.

Heat a separate pan over a high heat until it is as hot as possible. Place the lettuce halves in the pan, cut sides down, and cook for 1 minute, then drizzle with the olive oil and continue to fry for no longer than 1 minute. They will darken quite quickly without losing their raw texture.

Place the cooked lettuces on a serving platter, grilled sides up, and season with a little salt. Pour the hot vinaigrette over the top and enjoy.

ENSALADA DE SANDIA, ★ TOMATES Y QUESO ★

WATERMELON, TOMATO, CORIANDER AND GOAT CHEESE SALAD

SERVES 4

200G (7OZ) PEELED WATERMELON, SEEDED AND DICED

ABOUT 500G (1LB 2OZ) YELLOW OR HERITAGE CHERRY TOMATOES, HALVED

50G (2OZ) SOFT GOAT CHEESE

A FEW SPRIGS OF FRESH CORIANDER (CILANTRO), LEAVES SEPARATED AND FINELY CHOPPED

FOR THE VINAIGRETTE

1 GARLIC CLOVE, PEELED

A GOOD DRIZZLE OF BALSAMIC VINEGAR

½ RED ONION, THINLY SLICED

A HANDFUL OF BLACK OLIVES

A GOOD DRIZZLE OF EXTRA VIRGIN OLIVE OIL

A PINCH OF SEA SALT

Tomatoes are one of my top ingredients yet it is so hard to find good ones in non-sunny countries. Similarly, watermelon is in my top three fruits – so refreshing – and back in Spain they are so delicious. The mix of the two with the salty touch of the cheese makes a terrific salad.

For the vinaigrette, crush the garlic clove with the side of a knife and mix it with the balsamic vinegar in a small bowl. Add the red onion, olives and the oil. Leave to marinate.

Place the watermelon and tomatoes in a bowl. Crumble over the goat cheese and scatter with the coriander.

Drizzle the vinaigrette over the salad, scatter with sea salt and serve.

NOTE
If you want to add some leaves to this salad, I recommend rocket (arugula).

ENSALADA CALIENTE DE
★ CALAMAR, CHORIZO Y ENDIVIAS ★
PAN-FRIED SQUID WITH SPICY CHORIZO AND CHICORY SALAD

SERVES 4 AS A TAPA

4 SMALL OR 1 LARGE SQUID
(ABOUT 400G [14OZ]), CLEANED
(OR ASK YOUR FISHMONGER
TO DO THIS FOR YOU)

4 TBSP EXTRA VIRGIN OLIVE OIL

2 HEADS CHICORY (ENDIVE),
LEAVES SEPARATED

2 SPRING ONIONS
(SCALLIONS), THINLY SLICED

2 TOMATOES, CUT INTO WEDGES

1 SPICY COOKING (FRESH UNCOOKED)
CHORIZO, SLICED

2 TBSP SHERRY VINEGAR

SEA SALT

You have probably noticed how much squid there is in this book. Well, this is a true reflection of how much squid we actually eat in Spain. We love it in all its ways, not just in the ubiquitous deep-fried version. In this unusual salad you will find the saltiness of the pan-fried squid and chorizo combined with the bitterness of the chicory and the acidity of the sherry vinegar is a match made in heaven.

Prepare the squid by cutting it into small pieces and scoring the smooth flesh in a cross-hatch pattern.

Heat the oil in a frying pan over a high heat. Add the squid and a pinch of salt and fry the pieces on one side until golden, about 1 minute. Flip the squid and cook the other side (the total cooking time should be no more than 2 minutes).

Meanwhile, mix the chicory, spring onions and tomatoes together in a bowl.

Sauté the chorizo in a frying pan over a medium heat for a couple of minutes, until cooked. Remove from the heat and swirl the sherry vinegar in the pan.

Add the cooked chorizo and its vinegar, and the cooked squid to the salad and finish with a drizzle of olive oil and a sprinkling of sea salt.

★ ESGARRAET VALENCIANO ★

ROASTED RED PEPPER AND SALT COD SALAD

SERVES 6 AS A TAPA

450–500G (1LB) SALT COD

8 LARGE RED (BELL) PEPPERS

75ML (⅓ CUP) EXTRA VIRGIN OLIVE OIL,
PLUS EXTRA FOR DRIZZLING

2 LARGE GARLIC CLOVES,
THINLY SLICED

1 TSP BROWN SUGAR

SALT

FINELY CHOPPED FLAT-LEAF
PARSLEY, TO GARNISH

NOTE
The longer this dish
has to rest before
serving, the more
flavour it will develop.

Valencia is not just about paella. There is a very rich food culture, including this summery dish made with salt cod. Salted, shredded cured cod is easily found in the Jamaican section of any store, but Spanish or Icelandic salt cod is even better if you can find it. *Esgarraet* in Valencian means to shred, which is what we are about to do with this salad.

Soak the salt cod in cold water for 24 hours, changing the water 3 times during this time. Shred into small pieces with forks.

Preheat the oven to 220°C/425°F/gas mark 7.

Place the red peppers on a roasting tray and rub all over with the olive oil and some salt. Roast for 25 minutes, turning the peppers halfway through. Remove from the oven and transfer to a bowl of cold water, cover with plastic wrap and leave to rest for at least 30 minutes.

Discard the water from the bowl and use your fingers to peel away and discard the skin from the peppers. Tear the flesh into thick strips and place in the bowl with the juices.

Add the sliced garlic, a good drizzle of extra virgin olive oil, the sugar and the drained rehydrated salt cod. Garnish with the finely chopped parsley and serve.

ENSALADA DE FRISEE
★ Y GRANADA ★
FRISEE LETTUCE, POMEGRANATE AND OLIVE SALAD

SERVES 4

1 HEAD FRISÉE LETTUCE,
WASHED AND DRIED

1 X 200-G (7-OZ) TIN/JAR
SPANISH PITTED BLACK OLIVES,
ROUGHLY CHOPPED

1 POMEGRANATE

1 TBSP PUMPKIN SEEDS

FOR THE DRESSING

1 TSP SEA SALT

1 TSP HONEY

3 TBSP SHERRY VINEGAR

150ML (⅔ CUP) OLIVE OIL

I have discovered on my travels that in most countries bitterness is not a taste that is appreciated. In Spain, it is. A short time ago someone told me that most foods which are bitter are very good for the liver as they help to cleanse it and get rid of the bad stuff. Apparently we crave them without noticing. This salad couldn't be any more refreshing.

Chop the lettuce into small pieces, discarding the very bitter outer and greener leaves. Place in a salad bowl with the olives.

Cut off the top third of the pomegranate and scoop out the flesh and seeds with a spoon, capturing any juice in a small bowl for the dressing. Tap the scooped chunks over the salad bowl with the back of a spoon to release the seeds and discard the flesh. Squeeze any seeds that don't tap out into the dressing bowl with the juice. You want about 3 tablespoons pomegranate juice.

For the dressing, add the salt, honey and sherry vinegar to the pomegranate juice and whisk together to mix. Slowly pour in the olive oil in a steady stream, whisking constantly until the dressing emulsifies.

Dress the salad and sprinkle the pumpkin seeds over the top to serve.

SOPAS, LEGUMBRES Y ESTOFADOS

SOUPS, PULSES & STEWS

SOPA DE GUISANTES ★ CON JAMON ★

PEA SOUP WITH SERRANO HAM

SERVES 4

4 TBSP EXTRA VIRGIN OLIVE OIL

2 SLICES RUSTIC BREAD

3 GARLIC CLOVES, FINELY CHOPPED

1 ONION, FINELY CHOPPED

1 BAY LEAF

50G (2OZ) SERRANO HAM SLICES, FINELY CHOPPED, PLUS 4 EXTRA SLICES TO SERVE

1 TSP SWEET PIMENTÓN (SWEET SMOKED PAPRIKA)

1 TBSP PLAIN (ALL-PURPOSE) FLOUR

1 TBSP SHERRY VINEGAR

600ML (2½ CUPS) CHICKEN STOCK

500G (4 CUPS) FROZEN PEAS

SALT AND FRESHLY GROUND BLACK PEPPER

An amazingly warming, rich and healthy soup, this is made in just 20 minutes from start to finish. Frozen peas are so convenient and I reckon lots of people always have them in their freezer. No excuse not to try this one; I do it myself at home frequently.

Pour 1 tablespoon of the oil into a medium pan over a medium heat and fry the bread on both sides. Set aside.

Pour the rest of the oil into the pan, add the garlic, onion, bay leaf and the finely chopped ham and fry for 10 minutes.

Sprinkle over the sweet pimentón and the flour and let it cook for 1 minute, then pour in the sherry vinegar, stirring constantly, and cook for a couple of minutes to make a roux. Increase the temperature to high and continue to stir as you slowly pour in the chicken stock so that the roux dissolves in the stock without forming lumps. Add the frozen peas, season with salt and pepper and leave to boil for 6 minutes.

Top the sliced bread with the rest of the jamón ibérico and serve alongside the soup.

★ SOPA DE FIDEOS ★

NOODLE SOUP

SERVES 2

1 TBSP EXTRA VIRGIN OLIVE OIL

1 CHICKEN STOCK CUBE

A PINCH OF SWEET PIMENTÓN
(SWEET SMOKED PAPRIKA)

100G (3½OZ) FIDEOS OR ANGEL
HAIR PASTA

SALT AND FRESHLY GROUND
BLACK PEPPER

NOTE
You can find *fideos*
in the Jewish section
in supermarkets.
If you can't find them
just crush the thinnest
spaghetti you can
find between your
hands into 2–3-cm
(¾–1¼-in) pieces.

Every culture has something they eat when they
are sick or feel under the weather. The Chinese have
congee, for example, while others drink a soothing
tea. In Spain we have this simple broth with thin
pasta that feels like magic. I can't tell you how
many times I have eaten this.

In a small saucepan over a high heat, bring 600ml
(2½ cups) water, the oil, stock cube and sweet
pimentón to the boil. Whisk vigorously to dissolve
the stock cube completely.

Add the pasta and boil it all together for a couple
of minutes, or as per the manufacturer's instructions.
Season if needed and serve. Remember that the stock
cubes tend to be quite salty, so it may be that it doesn't
need any extra salt.

SOPA DE BACALAO, PUERRO, ★ MEJILLONES Y PATATAS ★

SALT COD, LEEK AND MUSSEL SOUP

SERVES 4

200G (7OZ) SALT COD, BONES REMOVED

3 TBSP EXTRA VIRGIN OLIVE OIL

1 LARGE ONION, ROUGHLY CHOPPED

2 GARLIC CLOVES, SLICED

3 LEEKS, THINLY SLICED

1 TSP SALT

3 POTATOES, CUT INTO BITE-SIZED CHUNKS

125ML (½ CUP) WHITE WINE

1 LITRE (5 CUPS) VEGETABLE STOCK

8 FRESH MUSSELS IN THEIR SHELLS

1 TBSP FRESH PARSLEY, CHOPPED, TO GARNISH

I love salt cod. It has so much depth of flavour and whatever you add it to it lends it a particular taste. Since this very comforting soup is water based, the cod infuses it intoxicatingly with a delicious aroma of the sea.

Soak the salt cod in cold water for 24 hours, changing the water 3 times during this time. Shred the flesh into small pieces.

Heat the oil in a saucepan over a medium heat and cook the onion and garlic until soft, about 5 minutes. Add the leeks and salt and cook for a further 15 minutes.

Add the potatoes and wine, increase the heat to high and let reduce for at least 2 minutes, then add the stock and simmer for about 25 minutes. Don't worry – the potatoes should be overcooked. Add the flaked salt cod and mussels and cook until the mussels open, about 3 minutes.

Garnish with the chopped parsley to serve.

★ SOPA DE MELON ★

CHILLED MELON SOUP

SERVES 4

1½ PIEL DE SAPO OR HONEYDEW MELONS, PEELED, SEEDED AND CUT INTO CHUNKS

2 MINT LEAVES

30G (1OZ) SERRANO HAM, VERY FINELY CHOPPED, TO SERVE, OPTIONAL

A DRIZZLE OF SINGLE (LIGHT) CREAM, OPTIONAL

OR

50ML (3½ TBSP) EXTRA VIRGIN OLIVE OIL

NOTE
To crisp up the ham, put it in the microwave on a plate and cook it for 30 seconds.

This is a summer dish that will refresh you in hot weather. It is normally eaten with Serrano ham shavings. However, you can omit it if you're cooking for vegetarians. In Spain, we use a local melon called 'piel de sapo'. Your soup will taste completely different depending on which type of melon you use, which, in my view, is all the fun.

Blend the melon chunks with the mint until you have a melon soup that is completely blended. Chill for at least 30 minutes in the fridge.

Give the chilled melon a good stir to bring it together again and serve, with the finely chopped ham and a drizzle of cream or extra virgin olive oil, if you like.

★ GAZPACHO DE SANDIA ★

CHILLED WATERMELON SOUP

SERVES 4

500G (1LB 2OZ) WATERMELON, PEELED AND CHOPPED

4 TOMATOES, CHOPPED

1 RED (BELL) PEPPER, CHOPPED

¼ CUCUMBER, CHOPPED

¼ ONION, CHOPPED

½ GARLIC CLOVE, CHOPPED

1 SLICE OF BREAD, CHOPPED

1 TSP SALT

1 TSP GROUND CUMIN

3 TBSP SHERRY VINEGAR

A DRIZZLE OF OLIVE OIL

This is a recipe that has been enjoyed by thousands of customers in my restaurants – incredibly tasty, so refreshing and full of goodness. In a nutshell, it is a blended salad. You can keep it in a bottle in your fridge for up to 3 days.

Place all the ingredients in a blender and liquidize until smooth. Check the seasoning and adjust if necessary. Serve over ice.

NOTE
If you want to serve this as a starter and make it a bit more filling, serve it in a soup bowl with croutons and a drizzle of extra virgin olive oil.

BACALAO CON
★ LENTEJAS SALTEADAS ★
COD AND LENTIL STEW

SERVES 4

7 TBSP OLIVE OIL

5 GARLIC CLOVES, THINLY SLICED

½ ONION, THINLY SLICED

2 RED CHILLI PEPPERS, CHOPPED

1 TSP SWEET PIMENTÓN
(SWEET SMOKED PAPRIKA)

1 X 410-G TIN (2 CUPS) COOKED
LENTILS, DRAINED

25ML (1 TBSP + 2 TSP) AMONTILLADO
SHERRY WINE

A HANDFUL FRESH FLAT-LEAF
PARSLEY, LEAVES SEPARATED

4 X 200-G (7-OZ) COD LOINS

SALT AND FRESHLY GROUND
BLACK PEPPER

A truly healthy dish, simply cooked with a convenient tin of cooked lentils. Across Castilla pulses are so popular, particularly as part of stews. We should all eat more pulses.

Heat 6 tablespoons of the oil in a pan over a medium heat and cook the garlic, onion and chilli until the onion is light golden. Sprinkle over the sweet pimentón and quickly add the lentils and sherry wine. Season with salt and pepper, add the parsley leaves, stir to combine and then immediately turn off the heat.

Add the remaining tablespoon of olive oil to another pan over a medium heat and cook the cod loins, skin side down, for about 5 minutes depending on the thickness of the loin, before flipping it over to finish cooking on the other side for a minute or so. Season to your liking.

Serve the cod loins with the lentils and a drizzle of olive oil on top.

★ CARNE GOBERNADA ★

BEEF STEW

SERVES 4

1 X 700–900-G (1½–2-LB) SHIN
(FORESHANK) OF BEEF

4 GARLIC CLOVES,
ROUGHLY CHOPPED

1 TBSP ROCK SALT

OLIVE OIL

1 LARGE ONION, ROUGHLY CHOPPED

1 RED (BELL) PEPPER,
ROUGHLY CHOPPED

1 GREEN (BELL) PEPPER,
ROUGHLY CHOPPED

1 CARROT, ROUGHLY CHOPPED

1 LEEK, ROUGHLY CHOPPED

1 TBSP SWEET PIMENTÓN
(SWEET SMOKED PAPRIKA)

120ML (½ CUP) WHITE WINE

1 LITRE (4¼ CUPS) BEEF STOCK

SOURDOUGH BREAD OR
FRIED POTATOES, TO SERVE

NOTE
In Spain we use pressure cookers a lot and they're very helpful for preparing these kinds of dishes. Try it – you could have this stew ready in half the time!

This is a very slow-cooked beef stew traditionally made in Asturias, northern Spain, and perfect for cold winter days. It is a simple recipe but it is essential to control the heat to get the flavours and textures right. Nowadays it's rarely found in Spanish restaurants and that's why I wanted to include it here. Who knows, perhaps it will become popular again! I like to prepare it the day before serving, and eat it with sourdough or fried potatoes.

Dice the meat and place it in a bowl with the chopped garlic, rock salt and a splash of olive oil and leave in the fridge for 24 hours.

The following day, remove the garlic from the meat. Heat 3 tablespoons olive oil in a large pan over a high heat and fry the beef for a couple of minutes to seal it. Add all the roughly chopped vegetables and cook for about 10 minutes. Once all vegetables are soft, add the sweet pimentón and mix well before adding the wine. Leave to cook until the liquid has reduced by half.

Add the beef stock, reduce the heat to a simmer and then cover and leave to stew slowly for at least 2 hours, or until the meat is tender. Check from time to time that you do not run out of liquid; you can add water if this happens.

Serve with sourdough bread or fried potatoes.

★ CAZUELA DE LANGOSTA ★

LOBSTER AND SAFFRON PASTA STEW

SERVES 4

400ML (1¾ CUPS) FRESH FISH STOCK, OR 1 FISH STOCK CUBE DISSOLVED IN 400ML (1¾ CUPS) WATER

1 TSP SAFFRON THREADS

4 TBSP EXTRA VIRGIN OLIVE OIL

½ ONION, FINELY CHOPPED

1 DRIED CAYENNE PEPPER (OR ANY OTHER DRIED RED CHILLI PEPPER)

1 BAY LEAF

1 LOBSTER

12 ROASTED ALMONDS, PEELED

2 TBSP BREADCRUMBS

3 GARLIC CLOVES

1 SALTED ANCHOVY

1 TSP TOMATO PURÉE (PASTE)

25ML (1 TBSP + 2 TSP) BRANDY

25ML (1 TBSP + 2 TSP) WHITE WINE

1 PIECE (10G [1½OZ]) DARK (BITTERSWEET) CHOCOLATE

100G (3½OZ) THIN 3-MINUTE SPAGHETTI, BROKEN INTO 3-CM (1¼-IN) PIECES

3 SPRIGS FRESH FLAT-LEAF PARSLEY, FINELY CHOPPED

SALT AND FRESHLY GROUND BLACK PEPPER

This dish is a real showstopper in terms of flavour. After I cooked it in under 8 minutes on national TV, all the guests were asking me, 'How did you make something so good in 8 minutes?' They couldn't believe it. Lobster is not cheap but for a special occasion, give this recipe a go.

Bring the fish stock to the boil in a large pan over a high heat and add the saffron. Allow to infuse for 10 minutes.

Meanwhile, pour the olive oil into a frying pan over a high heat and add the onion, cayenne pepper and bay leaf. Let it sizzle for a couple of minutes.

To prepare the lobster, cut the head in half lengthways and separate the head from the tail. Cut the tail horizontally into 2-cm (¾-in) (30-g [1-oz]) pieces. Twist off the claws but leave them whole. Add all the pieces to the pan.

Tip the almonds, breadcrumbs, garlic, anchovy and tomato purée into a small food processor and blend to a paste. Add to the pan.

Stir the pan for 1 minute and then flambé with the brandy and white wine. To do this, slowly tilt the pan towards the flame until the brandy catches, or light with a match. Let the flames flare up then die down and then add the boiling saffron-infused fish stock, the chocolate and pasta. Season with salt and pepper and leave to boil for 3 minutes until the pasta is al dente, the lobster is perfectly cooked and the clams have opened. Garnish with the parsley and serve.

★ POTAJE CANARIO ★

CANARY ISLAND MEAT AND VEGETABLE STEW

SERVES 6

2 GARLIC CLOVES, PEELED

½ BUNCH FRESH PARSLEY

EXTRA VIRGIN OLIVE OIL

4 FLOURY POTATOES

1 CARROT

1 ONION

150G (5¼OZ) MARROW OR COURGETTE (ZUCCHINI)

200G (7OZ) SQUASH, ANY KIND

300G (10½OZ) PORK RIBS (ASK YOUR BUTCHER TO CUT THEM INTO MEDIUM-SIZED PIECES)

2 CORN COBS, EACH CUT INTO 3 PIECES

1 TSP SMOKED PIMENTÓN (SWEET SMOKED PAPRIKA)

450ML (1¾ CUPS) MEAT OR VEGETABLE STOCK

100G (3½OZ) FLAT GREEN BEANS OR RUNNER BEANS

1 X 400-G TIN (1½ CUPS) CHICKPEAS (GARBANZO BEANS), DRAINED AND RINSED

100G (3½OZ) SPRING GREENS, ROUGHLY CHOPPED

SALT

As its name suggests, this stew is typical of the Canary Islands. Corn is well used there along with other more tropical produce (like mangoes, bananas, custard apples, pineapples) because of their climate and their South American heritage; historically, most journeys to the Americas had to stop in the Islands as it was the first pit stop after crossing the Atlantic and vice versa.

Use a pestle and a mortar to grind the garlic, parsley, a drizzle of olive oil and pinch of salt to make a paste and set aside.

Peel and roughly dice 1 of the potatoes, the carrot, onion, marrow or courgette and squash. Place all of these vegetables into a large stockpot together with the ribs, corn, the garlic paste and the pimentón. Add the stock, a drizzle of olive oil and enough water to cover all the ingredients and give it a good stir. Heat over a high heat and bring to the boil, then reduce the heat to medium-low and simmer for about 30 minutes, stirring from time to time. The potatoes will slowly break up and thicken the stew.

Meanwhile, peel the rest of the potatoes and dice them into 1.5-cm (½-in) squares. Remove the strings from the beans and cut each one into 4 pieces. Add to the pan with the chickpeas and spring greens and cook over a medium heat for a further 15 minutes. Turn off the heat, cover and leave to rest for another 15 minutes before serving.

RAGU DE CARRILLERAS ★ CON PASTA ★

STEWED PIG CHEEKS WITH PASTA

SERVES 4

500G (1LB 2OZ) PIG (PORK) CHEEKS, TRIMMED

75ML (⅓ CUP) EXTRA VIRGIN OLIVE OIL

½ LARGE ONION, DICED SMALL

½ CELERY STICK, FINELY CHOPPED

4 GARLIC CLOVES, FINELY CHOPPED

1 LARGE CARROT, FINELY CHOPPED

3 SPRIGS FRESH THYME

1 BAY LEAF

2 TOMATOES, QUARTERED

150ML (⅔ CUP) RED WINE

2 LITRES (2 QUARTS) CHICKEN STOCK

300G (10½OZ) PASTA SHELLS

SALT AND FRESHLY GROUND BLACK PEPPER

Pasta has been used in Spanish cooking for centuries due to the close links the east coast of Spain and the Balearic Islands had with Italy's west coast, Corsica and Sardinia. From Roman times we have always had a great cultural and trading relationship and good things, as good habits, spread fast. This pasta stew is rich and intense with so many layers of flavour that blend very well with the plain pasta.

Lightly season the pig cheeks with salt and pepper. Heat the olive oil in a large heavy-bottomed pan over a high heat and seal the cheeks on both sides. Remove the meat and set aside.

Add the onion, celery, garlic and carrot to the pan, adding more oil if necessary. Fry until dark golden and caramelized, about 8–10 minutes. Add the thyme, bay leaf and tomatoes and continue to cook for 5 minutes, then add the pig cheeks and red wine. Cook for 2 minutes to reduce the liquid, then pour in the stock, reduce the heat to medium and cook for 30 minutes. Reduce the heat again and leave to simmer for at least 2 hours, or longer, until the meat is tender.

Remove the pig cheeks from the pan and shred using a masher or fork. Return the shredded meat to the pan and simmer for a further 5 minutes. You will need enough liquid in the pan to cook the pasta with enough left for sauce. Add more water if necessary and add the pasta to the pan. Give it a good stir and cook over a low heat according to the packet instructions, until the pasta is al dente. The gluten released by the pasta should thicken the stew, giving it a great body and consistency. If it looks too dry, add more water halfway through cooking the pasta.

★ POTAJE MONTAÑES ★

CHORIZO, GREENS AND BEAN STEW

SERVES 6

350G (2 CUPS) DRIED BUTTER (LIMA) BEANS

500G (1LB 2OZ) PORK BELLY, CUT INTO 3-CM (1¼-IN) CHUNKS

3 SMOKED CHORIZO SAUSAGES (ABOUT 100G [3½OZ] EACH)

3 BLACK PUDDINGS (ABOUT 100G [3½OZ] EACH)

2 BAY LEAVES

4 TBSP OLIVE OIL

4 GARLIC CLOVES, THINLY SLICED

50G (2OZ) SERRANO HAM, DICED

1 TBSP PLAIN (ALL-PURPOSE) FLOUR

1 TSP SWEET PIMENTÓN (SWEET SMOKED PAPRIKA)

1 HEAD OF SPRING GREENS (OR ANY GREEN CABBAGE), ROUGHLY CHOPPED

I had only tried this dish once in my life before I cooked it for this book. I had it in the city of Santander with all my friends at the wedding of our dear friend Pablo. It was so good I have never forgotten about it. Note that you will need to soak the dried butter (lima) beans overnight before you start cooking.

Soak the dried beans in cold water overnight.

The next day, put the soaked and drained beans, pork belly, chorizo sausages, black puddings and bay leaves in a large saucepan and pour in about 3 litres (3 quarts) cold water.

Bring to the boil over a high heat then cook at a rolling simmer for 1 hour, skimming the froth that appears on the surface with the help of a ladle.

Pour the olive oil into a frying pan over a low heat and fry the garlic and Serrano ham for 5 minutes without getting any colour on them. Sprinkle the flour and pimentón into the pan and stir for a couple of minutes to form a roux.

Take a ladleful of liquid from the large saucepan and add it to the roux. Stir until combined and add another ladleful if necessary. Pour the contents of the frying pan into the large pan and stir. The roux will eventually make the stew a little thicker and have a better texture, instead of seeming like a soup.

Simmer for 2½–3 hours in total until the beans are soft, and add the spring greens 30 minutes before the end of the cooking time.

Serve in soup bowls, making sure everyone has equal portions of the different meats.

★ FABES CON ALMEJAS ★

CLAM AND BEAN STEW

SERVES 6

500G (3 CUPS) DRIED BUTTER
(LIMA) BEANS

1 ONION, CUT IN HALF

1 BAY LEAF

A PINCH OF SAFFRON THREADS

500G (1LB 2OZ) CLAMS, CLEANED
AND ANY OPEN OR DAMAGED
SHELLS DISCARDED

25G (1½ TBSP) BUTTER

1 TBSP EXTRA VIRGIN OLIVE OIL

A BUNCH OF SPRING ONIONS
(SCALLIONS), CHOPPED

4 GARLIC CLOVES, FINELY CHOPPED

1 TBSP PLAIN (ALL-PURPOSE) FLOUR

250ML (1 CUP) WHITE WINE

3 TBSP FINELY CHOPPED PARSLEY

SALT

NOTE
You can buy ready-cooked beans in a jar and you will have the same results in just 15 minutes.

This is another splendid example of a brilliant bean stew. Look for good-quality clams and pamper the beans – it is worth it.

Soak the dried beans in cold water overnight.

The next day, put the soaked and drained beans in a heavy-based saucepan with the onion and bay leaf. Pour in about 3 litres (3 quarts) cold water but do not add salt.

Bring to the boil over a high heat, skimming the froth that appears on the surface with the help of a ladle. Then, set the heat to low and simmer for at least 3 hours, until the beans are soft. Add the saffron after 1 hour and skim the surface from time to time. Reserve the cooking water.

Put the clams in a large bowl or in the sink, cover with cold salty water and leave for 1 hour, moving them around with your hand from time to time. This will help the clams to open and release any sand.

Melt the butter in a frying pan with the olive oil over a medium heat. Add the spring onions and cook until soft, then add the garlic and after a minute the flour. Stir it constantly for 2 minutes to toast the flour, then add the white wine. Give it a good last stir to prevent lumps from forming. Add the clams along with a couple of tablespoons of the bean cooking water, and the parsley.

Once the clams are open, mix everything together well and season to taste.

See photograph on page 142.

PAELLA Y ARROCES

PAELLA & RICE

★ PAELLA DE MARISCO ★

SEAFOOD PAELLA

SERVES 5

500G (1LB 2OZ) FRESH SQUID,
INNER PARTS REMOVED BUT KEPT
(YOU CAN ASK YOUR FISHMONGER
TO DO THIS FOR YOU)

50ML (3½ TBSP) EXTRA VIRGIN
OLIVE OIL

1 TBSP ROCK OR SEA SALT,
PLUS EXTRA FOR SEASONING

1 RED ROMANO OR BELL PEPPER,
CUT INTO THICK STRIPS

200G (7OZ) FLAT GREEN OR RUNNER
BEANS, CHOPPED (THIS IS OPTIONAL,
BUT I LIKE IT)

6 GARLIC CLOVES, FINELY CHOPPED

1 TSP SWEET PIMENTÓN
(SWEET SMOKED PAPRIKA)

2 TOMATOES (WEIGHING ABOUT
300G [10½OZ] IN TOTAL), GRATED

400G (HEAPED 2 CUPS) PAELLA RICE,
SUCH AS BOMBA, SENIA OR BAHIA

500G (1LB 2OZ) FRESH PRAWNS OR
LANGOUSTINES, OR A MIXTURE, A
FEW RESERVED WHOLE, OTHERWISE
HEADS AND SHELLS REMOVED

10 MUSSELS AND/OR CLAMS,
CLEANED AND ANY OPEN OR
DAMAGED SHELLS DISCARDED

How good this book is comes down to how good this recipe tastes. If you follow it, my friends and family say it is one of the very best paellas they have tasted. The intensity of flavour in the stock you make will be the most important thing, as well as how wide your paella pan is. Believe it or not, it makes all the difference. On a conventional hob at home, to achieve perfection you cannot cook a really good paella for more than three people. The caramelization of the ingredients and how the rice sears over the wide surface adds points to the flavour and end result. Having said all these things to satisfy the purists, for us home cooks (I include myself), if you cook it for more it still tastes amazing. I do it all the time.

To clean the squid at home, remove the inner parts with your fingers, cutting the inner core just above the tentacles. Don't discard any of these ugly parts as they will make a rich stock.

First make the stock (see next page for ingredients). Heat a good drizzle of extra virgin olive oil in a casserole dish over the highest heat. Add the head and shells of the prawns and langoustines and brown them for 2 minutes. Add the reserved inner parts of the squid, the carrot, onion, celery, leek, garlic halves, black peppercorns and bay leaf and let caramelize until the vegetables are a dark golden colour, then add the tomato. Cook for 2 minutes and then flambé with the brandy followed by the white wine. To do this, pour the alcohol into the dish and light with a match, keeping your head and hair well back. Let the flames flare up then die down. Continue to cook until the alcohol burns off and reduces down until completely gone, then add 3 litres (3 quarts) water and the fish bones or stock cubes.

Simmer the stock for no longer than 45 minutes, using a hand blender to blitz it after 30 minutes (yes,

Continued overleaf

FOR THE SHELLFISH STOCK

EXTRA VIRGIN OLIVE OIL, FOR FRYING

HEADS AND SHELLS OF 500G (1LB 2OZ) PRAWNS AND LANGOUSTINES (SEE PREVIOUS PAGE)

THE INNER PARTS OF THE FRESH SQUID (SEE PREVIOUS PAGE), INK INCLUDED

1 CARROT, ROUGHLY CHOPPED

1 ONION, ROUGHLY CHOPPED

1 CELERY STICK, ROUGHLY CHOPPED

1 SMALL LEEK, ROUGHLY CHOPPED

1 HEAD OF GARLIC, HALVED

3 BLACK PEPPERCORNS

1 BAY LEAF

1 TOMATO, ROUGHLY CHOPPED

50ML (3½ TBSP) BRANDY

120ML (½ CUP) WHITE WINE

3 WHITE FISH CARCASES OR 1 HEAD OF COD OR MONKFISH, OR 2 FISH STOCK CUBES

1G (2 TSP) SAFFRON THREADS

Recipe continued

shells and bones included) to extract as much flavour as possible out of every ingredient. After 45 minutes, pass through a very fine sieve into another pot. You should have about 2 litres (2 quarts) of intense, flavoursome shellfish stock. Add the saffron and reduce the heat to simmer until needed.

Roughly chop the squid tube, wings and tentacles.

Place your paella or wide frying pan over the highest heat with the olive oil, chopped squid and salt. Let the water from the squid evaporate before adding the red pepper and green beans, stirring constantly so that all the ingredients brown nicely. Add the garlic and stir for 1 minute before adding the sweet pimentón. Stir again and cook for 30 seconds, then add the tomatoes. If the garlic or pimentón start to burn, add the tomatoes a little earlier. Add the rice and stir for 2 minutes to sear the rice and give a slightly crispier bite to the end dish. It will also mean the rice loses less starch, making the grain feel looser. Pour over the hot stock and give everything a good stir, scraping the bottom of the pan to ensure all the caramelization is incorporated into the stock. Taste the seasoning at this point – it should taste very salty. Adjust if necessary.

The rice should be ready in about 18 minutes. Put your timer on and remember this will be the last time you stir the rice. Now it is time to let it cook on its own, we will only need to manage the heat. Let it simmer over the highest heat for 10 minutes, or until the liquid has reduced down to almost level with the rice, then reduce the heat to low and scatter the prawns, langoustines, mussels and/or clams over the top of the rice. Top with the reserved whole prawns. Season them lightly. They will steam gently above the paella.

Leave to cook for the remaining 8 minutes, until the water is gone and you can hear that the rice in the bottom of the pan is starting to fry. Put your ear close to the pan without burning your hair and let the paella talk to you. It should say, 'I am getting crispier on the bottom, this is good but don't let me burn please.'

After 5 minutes of resting time you should dig in. As the Spanish say, 'Rice doesn't wait for anyone; everyone should wait at the table for the rice to come.'

ARROZ DE COSTILLA
★ Y COLIFLOR ★

RICE WITH SAUSAGES, RIBS AND CAULIFLOWER

SERVES 6

50ML (3½ TBSP) OLIVE OIL

4 GARLIC CLOVES, PEELED

½ TBSP SWEET PIMENTÓN
(SWEET SMOKED PAPRIKA)

2 TOMATOES, CHOPPED

1G (2 TSP) SAFFRON THREADS

1 TBSP SALT

200G (7OZ) PORK RIBS,
CUT INTO PIECES ON THE BONE

200G (7OZ) FRESH PORK SAUSAGES,
CUT INTO 1-CM (⅜-IN) SLICES

½ SMALL ONION, FINELY CHOPPED

½ LARGE CAULIFLOWER,
BROKEN INTO FLORETS

500G (2⅖ CUP) PAELLA RICE,
SUCH AS BOMBA

1½ LITRES (6 CUPS + 4 TBSP)
BOILING WATER

Thanks to its humid weather, the Mediterranean capital Valencia is famous for its rice crops. Everyone in this part of Spain knows how to cook their rice in many different ways and this recipe is one of them. They like to show off, saying that they have a different rice recipe for every day of the month, which is actually the truth.

Heat the olive oil in a large casserole or pan over a medium heat. Fry the garlic cloves for 2 minutes until golden, then remove and purée with the pimentón, tomatoes, saffron and salt. Set this mixture aside.

Season the pork ribs and fry over a high heat in the same pan along with the sausages, until they are a dark golden colour. Add the onion and cauliflower florets and cook, stirring, for 3 minutes, then add the blended garlic mixture and fry over a medium heat for another 4 minutes to make a *sofrito*.

Add the rice to the pan, give it a good stir and then add the boiling water and cook over a high heat for 10 minutes, making sure the rice doesn't catch on the bottom of the pan. Reduce the heat to low and cook for a further 7 minutes, or until the rice is cooked and the water has evaporated, as if it was a paella.

★ ARROZ EN BLEDES ★

SOUPY RICE WITH SWISS CHARD AND BUTTER BEANS

SERVES 6

100ML (½ CUP) OLIVE OIL

1 SWEDE (RUTABAGA),
CUT INTO LARGE CUBES

4 SWISS CHARD LEAVES,
ROUGHLY CHOPPED

1 LARGE TOMATO, GRATED

1 TSP SWEET PIMENTÓN
(SWEET SMOKED PAPRIKA)

3 LITRES (3 QUARTS)
VEGETABLE STOCK

300G (2 CUPS) TINNED
BUTTER (LIMA) BEANS

1G (2 TSP) SAFFRON THREADS

500G (2½ CUPS) BOMBA
OR PAELLA RICE

SALT

It is a tradition in Spain to eat this dish on Father's Day, which is also Saint José (Joseph) saint's day (I remember because my mum is called Maria José, so we always celebrate this day with all the family), and the last day of Las Fallas de València, a huge celebration to commemorate Saint Joseph. So, it is a really important rice dish for the city.

Place the oil, swede and Swiss chard in a deep heavy-based casserole over a medium heat and cook for 5 minutes, stirring occasionally. Add the grated tomato and a pinch of salt and continue to cook for 4 minutes, then add the sweet pimentón, stir once and then immediately pour over the vegetable stock. Bring to the boil over a high heat and cook for 5 minutes, then lower the heat to medium and cook for a further 10 minutes.

Meanwhile, mash half the beans with the saffron and a little bit of the cooking stock, either with a fork or a mortar and pestle. Add both the mashed and whole beans to the casserole and stir well, as they can easily catch on the bottom of the pan. Add the rice and cook over a medium heat for a further 17 minutes, or until the rice is cooked. Give it a gentle stir every 3 minutes throughout cooking to help the starch bind the liquid together and give creaminess to the final dish. Taste and adjust the seasoning as needed before serving.

ARROZ MELOSO DE ★ GAMBAS Y ALCACHOFAS ★

CREAMY RICE WITH PRAWNS AND ARTICHOKES

SERVES 5

500G (1LB 2OZ) FRESH SQUID, CLEANED (YOU CAN ASK YOUR FISHMONGER TO DO THIS FOR YOU)

10 BABY ARTICHOKES, STALKS TRIMMED AND OUTER LEAVES REMOVED

50ML (3½ TBSP) EXTRA VIRGIN OLIVE OIL

1 TBSP ROCK OR SEA SALT

1 ONION, ROUGHLY CHOPPED

6 GARLIC CLOVES, FINELY CHOPPED

1 TSP SWEET PIMENTÓN (SWEET SMOKED PAPRIKA)

2 TOMATOES (WEIGHING ABOUT 300G [10½OZ] IN TOTAL), GRATED

1G (2 TSP) SAFFRON THREADS

2 LITRES (2 QUARTS) SHELLFISH STOCK (SEE PAGE 165)

400G (HEAPED 2 CUPS) SPANISH PAELLA RICE, SUCH AS BOMBA, BAHIA OR SENIA

500G (1LB 2OZ) FRESH PRAWNS, HEADS AND SHELLS REMOVED

This rice dish is a megahit in my restaurants. The artichokes give a beautiful liquorice flavour, which I love. People don't cook much with artichokes but I grew up with them. My mum used to just boil them whole and serve them with olive oil to dip in; it felt like a treat back then so I am a big fan.

Roughly chop the squid tube, wings and tentacles.

Cut the artichoke hearts into quarters and scrape away any of the furry choke with a teaspoon. (If you do this step in advance, squeeze over some lemon juice and keep them in cold water to stop them going dark and oxidizing.)

Place a large wide pan (or a big terracotta one if you have one) over a high heat and add the olive oil, squid and salt. Allow the squid to release its liquid and let it evaporate before adding the onion and artichoke, stirring constantly so that everything browns nicely.

Add the garlic and stir for 1 minute before adding the sweet pimentón. Stir again and cook for 30 seconds, then add the grated tomatoes. If the garlic or pimentón start to burn, add the tomatoes a little earlier. Add the saffron and stock and bring to the boil. Taste and adjust the salt if necessary; it should taste too salty at this stage as it will balance out once the rice is cooked.

Add the rice and cook for 5 minutes over the high heat, then reduce to low and continue to cook for 15 minutes, stirring every now and then. Add the prawn tails just 5 minutes before the rice is ready. The rice should have released a lot of starch with the stirring, making the texture thick and dense, like a risotto.

See photographs on following pages.

★ ARROZ MELOSOS DE SETAS ★

SOUPY RICE WITH MUSHROOMS AND COD

SERVES 5

200G (7OZ) SALT COD

2 LITRES (2 QUARTS) VEGETABLE OR BEEF STOCK

1 TSP SAFFRON THREADS

50ML (3½ TBSP) OLIVE OIL

1 TSP SALT

1 ONION, FINELY CHOPPED

½ RED (BELL) PEPPER, ROUGHLY CHOPPED

300G (4½ CUPS) WILD MUSHROOMS OR A MIX OF SHIITAKE AND OYSTER, CHOPPED OR TORN

5 GARLIC CLOVES, FINELY CHOPPED

1 TSP SWEET PIMENTÓN (SWEET SMOKED PAPRIKA)

1 TOMATO (ABOUT 150G [5½OZ]), GRATED

350G (HEAPED 1¾ CUPS) PAELLA RICE, SUCH AS BOMBA

This is a creamy paella that is cooked very differently to a dry paella like the Arroz de Costilla y Coliflor and Arroz del Senyoret on pages 167 and 174, where you don't stir the rice so that it doesn't release any starch. Here is the opposite: you want to stir frequently so that the starch gives a lovely creamy texture to the dish. I like to cook the rice until al dente as, by the time you plate it, sit down at the table and start eating, your rice should be just right. The end result for this dish will rely heavily on the quality and flavour that your chosen mushrooms give the stock, which will end up being absorbed by the rice.

Soak the salt cod in cold water for 24 hours, changing the water 3 times during this time. Shred it into small pieces.

When you are ready to start cooking, bring the stock to the boil and add the saffron to infuse. Turn off the heat.

Heat the oil in a large frying pan over a medium heat and add the salt, onion and red pepper. Cook for 5 minutes and then add the mushrooms and cook them for 10 minutes. Add the finely chopped garlic and cook for 1 minute before adding the sweet pimentón and after 20 seconds the grated tomato. Cook for another 3 minutes and then add the saffron-infused stock. Bring to the boil and add the rice. Give it a good stir and cook over a high heat for 10 minutes, stirring occasionally.

After 10 minutes, reduce the heat to low and add the shredded salted cod, then cook for 8 more minutes, stirring constantly, until the rice is al dente. Serve and eat right away.

★ ARROZ DEL SENYORET ★

LORD'S PAELLA, WITH SHELLFISH BUT NO SHELLS

SERVES 4

100ML (⅓ CUP) OLIVE OIL

1 TBSP SALT

2 FRESH SQUID (600G [1LB 5OZ] TOTAL), CLEANED (ASK YOUR FISHMONGER TO DO THIS) AND CHOPPED

½ SMALL ONION, VERY FINELY CHOPPED

5 GARLIC CLOVES, FINELY CHOPPED

1 TSP SWEET PIMENTÓN (SWEET SMOKED PAPRIKA)

1 TOMATO (WEIGHING 150G [5½OZ] IN TOTAL), GRATED

350G (1¾ CUPS) SPANISH PAELLA RICE, SUCH AS BOMBA

20 FRESH WHOLE KING PRAWNS (OR 20 LANGOUSTINES), HEADS AND SHELLS REMOVED

SALT

FOR THE SHELLFISH STOCK

HEADS AND SHELLS OF 20 PRAWNS (SEE ABOVE)

A DRIZZLE OF OLIVE OIL

1 LEEK, THINLY SLICED

1 CELERY STICK, THINLY SLICED

1 CARROT, THINLY SLICED

1 HEAD OF GARLIC, CLOVES SEPARATED AND FINELY CHOPPED

25ML (1 TBSP + 2 TSP) BRANDY

25ML (1 TBSP + 2 TSP) WHITE WINE

3 LITRES (3 QUARTS) FISH STOCK

1 SALTED ANCHOVY OR 1 TSP DRIED JAPANESE BONITO FLAKES OR 1 TSP THAI SHRIMP PASTE

6 BLACK PEPPERCORNS

1 BAY LEAF

1G (2 TSP) SAFFRON THREADS, TOASTED (SEE NOTE OPPOSITE)

This is a seafood paella for people who don't fancy getting their hands dirty peeling shellfish while they eat. *Senyoret* means 'lord' in the Valencian dialect and, back in the day, the lords wanted their food prepared and neat. This recipe relies heavily on the flavour of your fish stock. Ingredients in the Spanish Levante are of the highest quality and full of flavour, whether it is an onion or the fish they make the stock with. These ingredients are incomparable to the ones you find elsewhere sadly, but I have a solution. Whether you buy it or make it from scratch, you will need to give it extra flavour by adding more ingredients before you allow your rice to drink it. This is fundamental to any good rice dish or paella.

I believe that the only way to achieve the flavour that a master *arrocero* in Valencia will get into his paella is by making a shellfish stock with a previously made fish stock. I know it feels like you're doubling up but, seriously, it allows you to get good intensity and a depth that you will not achieve unless you do this.

Place the prawn heads and shells in a pan over a high heat with some olive oil. Add the leek, celery, carrot and garlic and cook until golden brown and there is an intense toasted shellfish aroma coming out of the pan.

Flambé with the brandy and wine. To do this, pour the alcohol into the pan and light with a match, keeping your head back. Let the flames flare up then die down, then immediately add the fish stock followed by the anchovy, peppercorns and bay. Simmer for 45 minutes.

Blend the stock to extract as much flavour as possible, then pass through a fine sieve. Pour into a pan over a low heat, add the saffron and simmer for at least 15 minutes.

Meanwhile, prepare the paella. Add the oil and salt to a large wide pan over a high heat and then add the squid. When it starts to pop a little bit, lower the heat to medium and add the onion. Fry for 5 minutes before adding the garlic. Continue to fry for about 1 minute, stirring constantly, then add the sweet pimentón and 20 seconds later the tomato. Fry altogether, stirring constantly, for about 4–5 minutes, or until the tomato has reduced down. Scrape the bottom of the pan while the tomato is cooking to release all the sticky bits.

Increase the temperature to its highest setting and add the rice. Give it a good stir to coat it in the *sofrito* and sear for 2 minutes. Pour in the boiling stock, give it a good stir and boil for 10 minutes. Do not stir the rice again or you will ruin the texture of your paella. After 10 minutes lower the heat to medium and check the seasoning for salt.

Roughly chop the prawn tails and scatter them over the pan, shaking the pan a couple of times to distribute them. Reduce the heat to low and cook for 8 minutes, or until the rice is cooked. Ideally a layer of toasted rice will form on the base of the pan, which unfortunately you cannot see but you can judge by the noise and smell – it should sound like it is crisping up and the smell should be toasty. Leave to rest for 5 minutes, then serve.

See photographs on following pages.

NOTE

You can add mussel meat or other shellfish to this rice, as long as it's cleaned from the shells.

NOTE

Saffron is the most expensive spice in the world and it's grown in just a few countries. Spanish saffron is regarded as the best and most expensive of all, partly because it is toasted and given an extra layer of flavour. As a result it loses weight, so it's even more precious, gram for gram. If your saffron is not Spanish I recommend you toast it before you use it. Wrap it in foil and hold it with a pair of tongs over an open flame for just 10 seconds, flipping the envelope every other second so that the heat is indirect and even and the saffron doesn't burn. It is extremely fine and delicate.

★ ARROZ AL HORNO ★

BAKED RICE WITH PORK RIBS AND SAUSAGE

SERVES 4

750ML (3¼ CUPS) CHICKEN, PORK OR BEEF STOCK

1G (2 TSP) SAFFRON THREADS

1 TOMATO OR 2 CHERRY TOMATOES, HALVED

1 HEAD OF GARLIC, SKIN ON, HALVED

300G (10½OZ) PORK RIBS OR SMOKED PANCETTA, CUT INTO SMALL PIECES

1 SMALL POTATO, CUT INTO 1-2-CM (⅜-¾-IN) CUBES

2 WHOLE MORCILLA (SPANISH BLOOD PUDDINGS), PREFERABLY MADE WITH ONION

4 CHIPOLATA SAUSAGES OR COOKING CHORIZO, CUT INTO SMALL PIECES

1 TSP SWEET PIMENTÓN (SWEET SMOKED PAPRIKA)

1 BAY LEAF

1 TOMATO, GRATED

350G (SCANT 2 CUPS) PAELLA RICE

150G (HEAPED 1 CUP) TINNED CHICKPEAS (GARBANZO BEANS), DRAINED

SALT

OLIVE OIL

This dish is even more popular in Valencia than paella and all my friends from the Mediterranean side of Spain say that it's Granny's star dish for family gatherings. It is worth using a terracotta pot to cook the entire recipe as it captures all the flavours from beginning to end, but you can use a pan or oven tray instead.

Preheat the oven to 200°C/400°F/gas mark 6.

Bring the stock to the boil in a saucepan. Add the saffron and let simmer while you prepare the rest of the ingredients.

Place a casserole dish, roasting tray or ovenproof frying pan over a medium heat and heat some oil. Fry the tomato and garlic halves until golden and set aside.

Add the ribs, potato cubes and all the sausages to the dish and cook for 15 minutes, until golden and roasted. Add the sweet pimentón, bay leaf, the grated tomato and salt to season, and fry carefully while stirring for 3–4 minutes. Add the rice and give all the ingredients a good stir. Cook over a medium heat for a further 2 minutes.

Pour the boiling stock into the dish along with the chickpeas and mix well, spreading the rice and meat around the whole dish. Place the garlic head and tomatoes on the top. Cook over the highest heat for 10 minutes and then transfer to the oven for a further 10 minutes.

Once the rice is cooked, leave it to rest for 3–4 minutes before serving in the centre of the table.

POSTRES Y DULCES

DESSERTS & SWEET TREATS

FRESAS AL BRANDY
★ Y CREMA DE QUESO ★

STRAWBERRIES POACHED IN BRANDY WITH A CHEESE CREAM

SERVES 4

300G (3 CUPS) STRAWBERRIES

5 TBSP CASTER (GRANULATED) SUGAR

25ML (1 TBSP + 2 TSP) BRANDY

GRATED ZEST OF 1 LIME

FOR THE CHEESE CREAM

400ML (2¼ CUPS) DOUBLE
(HEAVY) CREAM

1 VANILLA POD, SPLIT OPEN
LENGTHWAYS AND SEEDS SCRAPED

50G (¼ CUP) CASTER (GRANULATED)
SUGAR

40G (⅓ CUP) GOAT CHEESE

I love berries, and strawberries are my very favourites. I particularly like them with whipped cream. In this recipe, the strawberries have been lightly cooked and the whipped cream has a surprise addition. Together, they are such a treat.

For the cheese cream, place a small pan over a low heat and add the cream, vanilla pod and seeds, sugar and goat cheese. Bring just to the boil and then take off the heat and blend to a smooth cream. Set aside to cool.

Place the strawberries, 3 tablespoons of the sugar and the brandy in a small pan over a minimum heat. Cover and cook for 5 minutes, or until the sugar dissolves. Don't let it boil. Set aside to cool.

Mix the lime zest with the remaining 2 tablespoons sugar and spread out on a plate. Leave in a warm place to dry out.

Once the cheese cream has cooled down, use a whisk to whip it to the consistency of whipped cream.

Serve the poached strawberries topped with the cheese cream and sprinkled with the lime sugar.

See photograph on page 180.

★ HIGOS CON TETILLA ASADOS ★

BAKED FIGS WITH TETILLA CHEESE

SERVES 4

8 FIGS

1 CINNAMON STICK

200G (7OZ) TETILLA CHEESE
(OR ANY SOFT COW'S MILK CHEESE)

100G (½ CUP) SOFT BROWN SUGAR

25ML (1 TBSP + 2 TSP) SWEET SHERRY
WINE, PREFERABLY PEDRO XIMÉNEZ

A KNOB OF BUTTER

BREAD STICKS, TO SERVE

NOTE
For a really pretty
dish, cut a cross in
the top of each fig
and open them
out like flowers
before cooking.

Tetilla is a mild and creamy Spanish cheese that gets its name from its breast-like appearance (*tetilla* means breasts). I use it in this recipe because melted Tetilla is one of the most satisfying flavours, and because we all need a treat from time to time. Don't forget, food feels your soul!

Preheat the oven to 180°C/350°F/gas mark 4.

Slice the figs in half and place them in a roasting tray with the cinnamon stick. Break the cheese into pieces and spread it over the figs. Sprinkle with the sugar and the sweet sherry wine. Finish with a knob of butter and bake for 15–20 minutes.

Have some bread sticks to hand and enjoy this simple but very serious treat.

See photographs on following pages.

PIÑA ESTOFADA
★ CON RON Y CREMA DE COCO ★

POACHED CARAMELIZED PINEAPPLE IN RUM WITH A COCONUT CREAM

SERVES 3

3 TBSP CASTER (GRANULATED) SUGAR, PLUS 1 TSP

200G (1½ CUPS) CUBED PINEAPPLE

25ML (1 TBSP + 2 TSP) DARK RUM

50G (¼ CUP) COCONUT CREAM

100ML (½ CUP) DOUBLE (HEAVY) CREAM

1 TSP MUSCOVADO SUGAR

This is a recipe I learned from my years with Ferran Adrià. It was a very refined dish, as you would expect, served during the summer in a Martini glass with all sorts of foams and innovative touches. This is my stripped-back version, full of flavour and very simple to make.

Place a pan over a high heat and sprinkle over the 3 tablespoons sugar. Cook until caramelized and dark, about 4 minutes, then add the pineapple cubes and sauté. Add 100ml (⅓ cup) water and the rum to the pan and let simmer over a low heat for about 5 minutes. Chill.

In a separate bowl whip the coconut cream, the teaspoon sugar and the double cream. Pour a little of the caramelized pineapple into a cocktail glass and top with the coconut whipped cream. Sprinkle with muscovado sugar to finish off.

★ CREMOSO DE CHOCOLATE ★

CHOCOLATE GANACHE WITH OLIVE OIL AND SALT

SERVES 4

5 GELATINE LEAVES

100ML (½ CUP) DOUBLE
(HEAVY) CREAM

100ML (¼ CUP) MILK

180G (1 CUP) CHOPPED DARK
(BITTERSWEET) CHOCOLATE
(70% COCOA SOLIDS)

GRATED ZEST OF ¼ ORANGE

A DRIZZLE OF EXTRA
VIRGIN OLIVE OIL

A PINCH OF SEA SALT

This a straightforward chocolate ganache with two very distinctive Spanish twists: olive oil and orange. It can also be used as a filling in a blind-baked pastry case, or for making good truffles.

Soak the gelatine leaves in cold water for at least 10 minutes, then drain, squeezing out all the excess water.

Bring the cream and milk almost to boiling point in a small pan over a medium heat. Take off the heat and add the chopped chocolate, orange zest and gelatine leaves and stir with a spatula, whisk or blender until completely dissolved. Chill in the fridge for 4 hours until completely set.

Serve in little pots, and dress with a drizzle of extra virgin olive oil and a pinch of salt to serve. You could also crumble some biscuits to eat it with or even serve it with strawberries.

FRUTAS SECAS AL JEREZ
★ CON CREMA DE MANCHEGO ★

DRIED FRUITS STEWED IN SHERRY WINE WITH
A MANCHEGO CHEESE GANACHE

SERVES 6

150G (¾ CUP) CASTER (GRANULATED) SUGAR

500ML (2 CUPS) PEDRO XIMÉNEZ SWEET SHERRY WINE

200G (1½ CUPS) PITTED DATES

200G (1½ CUPS) CURRANTS

200G (1½ CUPS) PITTED PRUNES

400ML (2¼ CUPS) DOUBLE (HEAVY) CREAM

200G (7OZ) MANCHEGO CHEESE, CHOPPED

100G (½ CUP) CREAM CHEESE

A HANDFUL OF PISTACHIOS, CHOPPED

In Spain we grow a lot of vegetables and fruits. We supply a good proportion of the whole of Europe's fruit and veg. In the old days exporting was not as easy as it is now and we had to make sure nothing went to waste. A lot of the dried fruits in Spain are made with summer fruits that after the sun-drying process are then enjoyed in winter, particularly at Christmas. This recipe brings them back to life and the salty cheese ganache makes a good balance with the sweetness of the stewed fruits.

Heat a small pan over a medium heat and sprinkle over 100g (½ cup) of the sugar. Add the wine and all the fruit and simmer gently for 1 hour. The fruit will absorb the richness of the wine and soften.

In a separate pan bring the cream, cheeses and the rest of the sugar just to boiling point, stirring constantly with a whisk, and then take off the heat. Blend until smooth and then put back over the heat, whisking constantly until the mixture comes back to the boil. Blend again until very smooth. Chill in the fridge until cold and then whip with a whisk until the mixture acquires the texture of whipped cream.

Serve the fruit with a little of the sherry syrup and a spoonful of the Manchego cheese ganache on top. Sprinkle with a few chopped pistachios and serve.

★ ENSAIMADA MALLORQUINA ★

ROLLED FLAKY PASTRY

SERVES 4

7G (SCANT 1 TSP) DRIED YEAST

200G (1 CUP) CASTER
(SUPERFINE) SUGAR

2 MEDIUM EGGS

600G (4¼ CUPS) VERY STRONG FLOUR

A PINCH OF SALT

100G (SCANT ½ CUP) LARD

3 TBSP ICING (CONFECTIONERS')
SUGAR

VEGETABLE OIL, FOR GREASING

OPTIONAL FILLINGS

50G (2OZ) SOBRASADA DE
MALLORCA (SEE PAGE 84) MIXED
WITH 50G (SCANT ¼ CUP) LARD

OR

200ML (¾ CUP) WHIPPED CREAM
OR CRÈME PÂTISSIÈRE

This is one of the most iconic pastries in Spain. It has earned such a renowned status because it is delicious, not just in flavour but in texture, too. The secret is in the way the pastry is made. By rolling it over itself, you achieve really thin layers once it's baked (like a croissant) and it's a treat to dig into.

Pour 230ml (1 cup) water into a bowl and add the dried yeast. Allow to dilute and then add the caster sugar, eggs, flour and salt. Mix together to form a dough and then knead for a good 15 minutes, until the dough is so elastic you can almost see through it if stretched. Set aside to rest for 30 minutes, then cut into 4 equal pieces and leave to rest for another 30 minutes.

Grease the work surface and a rolling pin with vegetable oil. Flatten one of the dough portions against the worktop with the palm of your hand and roll it out to a very thin rectangle about 20 x 60cm (8 x 24in). Let rest for 2 minutes while you spread a quarter of the lard over it with your fingers. Now, grab a corner of the flattened dough and stretch it out as far as it will go without breaking and repeat every 10cm (4in) or so around the dough in every direction until you have a rectangle about 50 x 70cm (20 x 28in).

Cut a 5-cm (2-in) strip from one of the long sides of the rectangle and place it over the end of the perpendicular side of the rectangle (this is what we call the heart of the *ensaimada*). Since this style of dough, like pizza dough, is always slightly thicker around the edges, it helps to have an extra layer of dough in the very heart of the pastry to provide some extra

NOTE
To achieve the right conditions to prove the pastries I wet 2 pieces of kitchen paper, cut them into pieces, roll into balls and place around the pastries and in the corners of the baking sheet. I place a deep roasting tray upside down over the pastries, wrap them in plastic wrap and leave somewhere fresh.

thickness. Additionally, when it bakes, the heart remains doughy and moist – delicious! Wrap a thin layer of dough over the heart and keep rolling it over itself until you have a long pastry snake. Repeat with the remaining portions of dough.

Grab the first roll of pastry you made and stretch it until it is over a metre (40in) long. Then roll it up in a spiral, leaving 1cm (½in) between each spiral. Flatten a little and transfer to a baking sheet lined with baking parchment. Repeat with the remaining pastries. Leave in a humid, fresh (14°C/57°F) and enclosed environment for no more than 12 hours. You will know it is ready when the pastry coils have risen and expanded enough to stick together.

When you are ready to start baking, preheat the oven to 200°C/400°F/gas mark 6. Put the baking sheet in the top third of the oven and immediately lower the temperature to 180°C/350°F/gas mark 4. Bake the pastries for about 15 minutes with heat top and bottom and the fan running, until the pastries are a dark golden colour. Cool on a wire rack and then dust with a generous amount of icing sugar.

If you want to fill your pastry with Sobrasada de Mallorca, use the Sobrasada-lard paste in the same way we used the lard in the main recipe method. It gives a fantastic savoury result.

To fill your *ensaimada* with whipped cream or crème pâtissière, cut open the baked pastry, spread it with the cream, sprinkle with sugar and caramelize with a blow torch before closing.

See photographs on following pages.

★ TURRON DE ALMENDRA ★

ROASTED ALMOND NOUGAT

MAKES 1 BAR

300G (2⅕ CUPS) GOOD-QUALITY
RAW ALMONDS, IDEALLY SPANISH,
SUCH AS MARCONA, SKINLESS

1 EGG WHITE

200G (¾ CUP) HONEY

100G (⅛ CUP) CASTER
(SUPERFINE) SUGAR

½ TSP GROUND CINNAMON

Let's talk about Christmas. In Spain we have some of the same traditions as in the UK and US, but different ingredients: Spanish Christmas songs, food and, of course, sweets. In all homes across Spain, we have *turrón* to finish a copious dinner. You could say that *turrón* is the Spanish fruit cake.

Preheat the oven to 200°C/400°F/gas mark 6.

Spread the raw almonds over an roasting tray and roast them for 3–4 minutes, until lightly golden. Set aside to cool, then crush in a food processor. Be careful not to pulverize the almonds as they will release juices and oils that are needed for a good consistency later on.

Whisk the egg white in a clean, grease-free bowl until it is an opaque white foam. This will take a few minutes with an electric whisk or in a mixer.

Put the honey, sugar and cinnamon into a heavy-based pan over a low-medium heat and stir with a wooden spoon or spatula until the sugar has melted with the honey. Remove from the heat and add the egg foam, little by little, whisking and mixing continuously. Place the pan back over a low heat and add the crushed almonds, a little at a time, still stirring and mixing with a wooden spoon or a spatula as the mixture thickens, for no longer than 5 minutes.

If your mixture splits for some reason, you can blend this mix in the food processor again for 30 seconds and it will come back together.

Pour the mixture into a rectangular silicone mould or a baking tin (about 25 x 12cm [10 x 5in]) lined with baking parchment, and use a spatula to push and spread the mixture level and into the corners. Cover with parchment paper and rest a heavy bag of rice or similar on top to weight it down. Let set in a cold environment for at least 24 hours.

★ MELOCOTONES AL MOSCATEL ★

PEACHES POACHED IN MUSCATEL WINE

SERVES 4

4 PEACHES, HALVED AND STONED (NECTARINES OR APRICOTS WORK AS WELL)

350–500ML (1½–2 CUPS) SWEET MUSCATEL WINE

½ CINNAMON STICK

2 STAR ANISE

5 JUNIPER BERRIES

ICE CREAM, CLOTTED CREAM OR NATURAL YOGURT, TO SERVE, OPTIONAL

In Spain, we love to remain at the table once we have finished eating. This is what we call *sobremesa*, chatting and chatting before the siesta arrives. A sweet wine such as Muscatel is the perfect ingredient to end a proper meal. This recipe includes fruit and this fantastic sweet wine combined. Try it!

Place the halved peaches in a deep pan; ideally they should fit snuggly, holding each other. Add the Muscatel, cinnamon, star anise and juniper berries and cook over a high heat until boiling, then immediately reduce the heat and simmer for 10 minutes, or until the peaches start to soften up. Don't overcook them; they should still be firm. Remove from the heat and leave to cool in the liquid, preferably overnight. This will help the flavours to develop within the fruit.

These peaches can be served with a wide range of accompaniments, such as ice cream, clotted cream or natural yogurt, for a more substantial dessert.

FLAN DE NARANJA
★ Y ALMENDRA ★

ORANGE AND ALMOND CREME CARAMEL

SERVES 8

400G (2 CUPS) CASTER
(GRANULATED) SUGAR

300ML (1¼ CUPS) DOUBLE
(HEAVY) CREAM

150G (1¼ CUPS) BLANCHED ALMONDS

GRATED ZEST AND JUICE OF 1 ORANGE

5 WHOLE EGGS

8 EGG YOLKS

A MOULD ABOUT 30CM (12IN)
IN DIAMETER

This is such a treat of a dessert and even though it comes without a photograph you should definitely try it. It couldn't be any easier to make as you only need to blend all the ingredients in a jar. If there is a dish that visually tells you to 'eat me', it would be this one, as it has the most beautiful golden and custardy colour once it's cooked.

Preheat the oven to 135°C/275°F/gas mark 1.

To make the caramel, put 100g (½ cup) of the sugar and 2 tablespoons water in a small saucepan over a medium heat. Tilt and swirl the saucepan gently when parts of the sugar start to turn into caramel so that it all cooks homogeneously and no part of it burns. When you have a caramel that is dark golden and just starting to smoke very slightly, pour it into the mould and swirl it to coat the bottom and sides. Allow the caramel to cool while you make the rest of the mixture.

Put all the remaining ingredients, including the remaining 300g (1½ cups) sugar in a blender and blitz for about 1 minute.

Pour the mixture into the mould and cover it with foil. Place it in a roasting tray filled with a 1-finger depth of cold water, to create a bain marie.

Bake in the preheated oven for about 40 minutes, or until set. Allow to cool and set completely in the fridge.

When you are ready to serve, run a paring knife around the inside of the mould. Make sure the crème caramel has come loose from the mould before covering it with a plate and flipping it over to release it.

★ GALLETAS DE ACEITE ★

OLIVE OIL, RAISIN AND LEMON COOKIES

SERVES 4

125G (⅔ CUP) CASTER (SUPERFINE) SUGAR

100G (½ CUP) BROWN SUGAR

150ML (⅔ CUP) EXTRA VIRGIN OLIVE OIL

1 TSP VANILLA EXTRACT

1 EGG

100G (¾ CUP) RAISINS

½ TSP SALT

GRATED ZEST OF 1 LEMON

250G (1¾ CUPS + 2 TBSP) SELF-RAISING FLOUR

I created this recipe one day when I was searching for a good cookie that differed from traditional American flavours. It had to be healthier and encapsulate the taste of Spain. If you travel around Spain, pretty much wherever you are, on either side of the road you will see vineyards, olive groves and citrus trees. It didn't take me long to work out what my cookie had to taste like.

In a big bowl, vigorously whisk both the sugars with the olive oil for 2 minutes. Add the vanilla extract and the egg and whisk for another 2 minutes. Add the raisins, salt and lemon zest. Sift over the flour and fold with a spatula for no longer than 2 minutes. The mixture will lose its fluffiness and get firmer the longer you fold it, so don't overdo it. Chill the dough in the fridge for 30 minutes.

Preheat the oven to 180°C/350°F/gas mark 4 and line a baking sheet with parchment paper.

Roll the chilled dough into balls the size of ping pong balls and place on the prepared baking sheet, leaving at least 10cm (4in) between each one to allow for spreading. Bake for about 7 minutes if you like them soft and doughy, or 9 minutes if you prefer them crispier.

★ INDEX ★

★ ACKNOWLEDGMENTS ★

I write this with a big smile on my face and tears in my eyes because I am so thankful and feel so fortunate to have in my life the people that I do.

The last couple of years have been a rollercoaster but I am so happy with how things have worked out. Thanks to all of you the future looks brighter than ever.

Familia, gracias por todo vuestro apoyo y amor incondicional. Aunque estemos muy unidos se os hecha mucho de menos desde la distancia. Especial mencion para mis padres y hermano que me habeis dado siempre todo lo mejor y habeis velado por mi, lo tengo presente en cada minuto de mi vida, es mi sostento y mi energía vital. Os quiero.

Dani, gracias por tu ayuda y amistad, indudable-mente todo es más llevadero a la par! Jaja

Ken, Douglas and Mac, thank you for being so supportive. It's a pleasure and an honour for me to work with you. I couldn't ask for more.

Magal and Louisa, thank you for all your help. You know what it means to me and I'll be eternally grateful.

Sarah, hooray, we did it again! For the record, you and Céline are the toughest colleagues I have ever had in my life, and I have never been chased to get a job done like that before. You kept me awake from tension for so many nights! But seriously, thank you for believing in me from the start. I am so glad you are as crazy as I am for giving me a second chance – what a relief I am not alone. It's such a pleasure to work with you and your professionalism is appreciated.

The Smiths and the Gilmours, this second time around certainly has the extra dimension we were all looking for and we felt was necessary. It feels even more Spanish and I love the results. Thank you so much – it looks terrific. I am so glad we shared pages again.

Martin, Martin, Martin… like a good Rioja, you just get better with time, don't you? I seriously thought the first book was unbeatable in terms of photography but you did it again, mate. I am so impressed. Thank you so much for making my food shine and for the fun.

Rosie, Sian and Polly, thank you for making the recipes look as they meant to, which wasn't an easy task at all. We aimed high and I feel we achieved it – cracking job.

Publishing director: Sarah Lavelle
Creative director: Helen Lewis
Senior editor: Céline Hughes
Art direction and design: Smith & Gilmour
Photography: Martin Poole
Food stylist: Rosie Reynolds
Food stylist assistant: Sian Henley
Props stylist: Polly Webb-Wilson
Production: Tom Moore, Vincent Smith

This edition published in 2021 by Quadrille, an imprint of Hardie Grant Publishing

Quadrille
52–54 Southwark Street
London SE1 1UN
quadrille.com

Text © 2016 Omar Allibhoy
Photography © 2016 Martin Poole
Design and layout © 2016 Quadrille

Cataloguing in Publication Data: a catalogue record for this book is available from the British Library.

ISBN: 978 1 78713 7202

Printed in China

FSC
www.fsc.org

MIX
Paper from responsible sources
FSC™ C020056